ON THE RUN

ON THE RUN

THE LIFE AND ADVENTURES
OF A FUGITIVE

by
Douglas McHardie

A Craven Street Book
Linden Publishing
Fresno, CA

ON THE RUN
by
Douglas McHardie

This edition
Copyright (c) 2003 Linden Publishing Inc.

135798642

Printed in United States of America

ISBN: 0-941936-80-5

Library of Congress Cataloging-in-Publication Data
McHardie, Douglas, b. 1882.
  On the run : the life and adventures of a fugitive / by Douglas McHardie.
      p. cm.
Originally published: London : S. Low, Marston & Co., 1936.
ISBN 0-941936-80-5 (pbk. : alk. paper)
1. McHardie, Douglas, b. 1882. 2. Adventure and adventurers--Biography.
I. Title.
CT9971.M39A3 2002
910'.92--dc21

2003001300

Originally published circa 1936 by Sampson Low, Marston & Co. London.

A Craven Street Book
Linden Publishing
2006 S. Mary
Fresno Ca 93721
www.lindenpub.com

AUTHOR'S FOREWORD

Na pah zor, na pah zarey, na pah jang.
Hes sok d'bul sarey naseeb miloegi bah
hes na rang.
Pushtu Proverb.

A man must pursue his own destiny.
Nor by force, by fight, by plot
Nor the hand of another
Can he alter it one iota.

THIS has been a difficult book to write, for I feel I have not conveyed to the reader that my life has been, and still is for that matter, as much an adventure of my mind as my mere actions. I am anxious not to be too easily condemned on the face of deeds, and there are many—bad ones. After all, what does the average person know of those they call bad? I have a theory that unless you have met them, the real "bad men", it is impossible to judge. Being criminal is so often a case of time, place and situation. What is condemned in Asia is approved in Europe and vice-versa. When, therefore, the reader learns that I have spilt blood, which I have often enough, perhaps wantonly, let him take into account all the circumstances before he brands me killer.

At one period of my life, in India, I am certain that I experienced the existence of a second personality, and though I am aware that dual personality is sometimes scoffed at as a theory, I have *lived* it in fact. But all the memories remain. Deal lightly with me in your thoughts, then, remembering I have lived as the person I was, wherever I have been. I have gone too long in fear of my life to be afraid of blood—even the blood of men. The first time I had it on my hands it was not the sight but the smell which bothered me. It reminded me of the first sheep I killed when I was just a kid. Even that now means little enough—perhaps wrongly. Maybe I am cursed, for I must make a last assertion before you read the story of its contradiction at every turn of my life. Since the day I left home I have sought in my heart one thing—peace! I have known most things at some time, wealth, comfort, poverty, hardship and the love of women; but peace has been denied me. Perhaps it always will be. But even now I have not lost hope. I shall go on imagining it to be always—just round the corner.

CONTENTS

vii

ON THE RUN

CHAPTER I

COWBOY

I

First and last I had better state clearly that there is little of the romantic in running away from home. I have talked to a good many runaways since I took the road myself and without exception they have all endorsed my opinion. The powder-monkey to admiral and bootblack to millionaire gentry will invariably be found on examination to have burgeoned in happy, even if humble, homes. . . .

Any sort of domestic life which proves so unendurable, that the son of the house at last finds uncontrollable his fierce desire to escape, wreaks such psychological havoc in the youthful mind that any question of a settled life for ever after becomes irksome. It was in no spirit of high adventure that I stole furtively away into the night. I was utterly wretched and sick at heart.

My father was a red-haired giant of a Scot who had found or fought his way gradually across the

United States to the lumber camps of upper California and Oregon, and it was in the small town of Humboldt in the former state that I was born in the year 1882. How such a man as my father ever came to be married I have never discovered, for home in the accepted sense was something for which he had precious little use. The kindly, patient soul who was my English mother seems even more inexplicable to me, for it was unquestionably a first-class *mésalliance*.

We worked a small-holding in the town which kept my mother and myself in the bare necessities of life, for we saw my father rarely enough. Most of the time he was logging and prospecting up in Eureka, in the giant redwood forests, and when he had earned sufficient money to visit his family again, it was his invariable custom to arrive home fighting drunk! It was on the occasions of these visits that I received the little education which was to carry me through life. Learning was no hardship to me since hard work was all I knew since the time I was knee-high to a duck. Nevertheless I am bound to give my father his due in that he was no fool. I have heard since that even elementary schooling in Scotland many years ago reached a standard to which it took many years for other countries to conform. I have no reason to grumble, therefore, at what I was taught. It was the manner of teaching. For in addition to a heavy hand my father had a

tongue which stung worse than any lash. I don't
suppose I was a paragon among pupils in any case,
but I had the will to learn, at least. Nothing, however, could be learned quickly enough to please my
father. He would call me a fool in all the many
ways he knew, until at last I developed what in
these days is termed an "inferiority complex". I
began to believe what he said, and that I was, in
fact, stupid and ignorant, that I would never be
able to support myself when I grew to manhood;
that I hadn't, in my father's own terms, the brains
of a louse.

His sarcastic sneer began to haunt my dreams.
It was not the two hundred pounds of muscular
Scotsman I feared, but the bitter contempt in which
he evidently held me. I had compensation in my
mother, only to be shunned for fear of fulfilling my
father's prophecy that I should be tied for ever to
her apron-strings. Sometimes he would take me
with him on hunting expeditions and I would thrill
at the thought of an opportunity to exhibit my
ability in at least one direction. But even that was
denied me, for the trip would usually degenerate
into endless sessions in the saloons on the way.
There was nothing my father loved more dearly
than a fight, and to his credit let it be said that
the only one he lost was his last, and that he died
in. These brawls were usually about Scotland, I
remember. Woe betide the man who dared to

suggest that it was anything but an earthly Paradise populated by a race of super-men, such as himself, called Scotsmen! The trouble invariably began in the same way. Some pot-valiant in the bar would have the temerity to demand why the hell my father didn't go back there if it was such a darned good place to live in? Then the trouble would start. It didn't usually last very long. My father would complacently order another drink standing over the body of his vanquished opponent. He bore no ill-will. "The man canna fecht so guid," he would say, and there the matter ended.

It was the cumulative effect of witnessing so many of these feats of strength and the fear and hatred which I held in my heart for this great man that made me take a childish oath to myself that I would one day be a better man than him. I was already a pretty husky kid. I would swear stronger, drink more, and be a better fighter. There was no thought, mind you, of living a better life. My standard of values was founded on those of my father. I was sixteen years old when I first tried to prove that I was already the better man. His manner had been particularly provoking one evening and he had sneered at me for a contemptible good-for-nothing once too often. Greatly daring, I lost my temper and rushed at him.

You might imagine, perhaps, that this display of spirit would please such a man. Nothing of the sort. He nearly killed me for my lack of respect, and when I eventually recovered announced his intention of murdering me if I didn't get to hell out of his sight immediately.

II

That night, burning with rage and resentment, I made up my mind to take him at his word. Even the thought of leaving my mother would not deter me. He had bruised my pride once too often. In my locked room I heard him stumble in from the saloon at midnight and climb the stairs of our little house. I knew he would be asleep in less than five minutes. He was rarely capable on such occasions even of undressing. In a teapot on the kitchen dresser I knew were three silver dollars. I crept downstairs, took the money and left the house, as I thought, for ever. I seemed to throw a great weight from myself as I breathed the cool night air.

By dawn I was nearly fifteen miles from Humboldt, and sufficiently cooled to begin to wonder what I was going to do. By seven o'clock I had bought myself a loaf of bread and a substantial piece of sausage, and become possessed of the vague idea of heading south. Several boys in the neighbourhood had gone down into the ranch country, and from all accounts it was simple enough to get a job on a ranch. And since I had been able to ride since I was a kid that aspect of suitability presented no obstacles. Before that could be achieved, however, there was a journey of some hundreds of miles and the prospect of crossing the Sierra Nevada, somehow. I was not particularly inclined to walk, and the automobile at that date was merely an engineer's dream. Horses must be stolen, and in spite of my upbringing I still possessed at that date a healthy regard for the law. But question answered itself soon enough. A man, whose generally unpleasant appearance stamped him unmistakably as a hobo, was trudging along in front of me bearing a can, which I subsequently discovered contained water. My mind was made up instantly. After all, I considered, these fellows seemed to do pretty well for themselves. I had heard tales that they covered immense distances every year. They knew the secret of riding the rails. It would be useful to me. I determined to learn it.

I must confess it was not without a certain trepidation that I caught the man up and spoke to him.

"Where are you going, fella?" I asked.

He stopped and surveyed me critically.

"You on the bum?" he countered.

"Sure," I told him. "But I only just started, I guess."

Evidently my manner convinced him, since he said: "Got any grub?"

I shewed him my loaf and sausage.

"O.K., buddy," he told me. "You c'n muck in with that over at the jungle."

In the shelter of a clump of trees a little farther up the road we came to the "encampment," and what little self-assurance remained to me ebbed even lower. One or two of the company I was pleased to see were not much older than myself, but they already bore the hard-bitten, dogged expression which, I suppose, I was soon to assume myself. The majority of the men were old stagers, dyed-in-the-wool hoboes, booze-sodden, vicious, lazy. Here and now I can explode the theory of the brotherhood of the road which has been served up in seven-and-sixpenny editions quite frequently lately. There is no more brotherhood among such men than there is honour among thieves. It is every man for himself. They submit to occasional communal life at the hobo camps merely in the general interest of self-preservation. Even there life is to the strong. One thing, however, I will say for them. If you rate as a bona-fide hobo, you may eat from the common pot without the necessity of contributing. It is unwritten law that a man will give what he can when he can. And that is where the brotherhood begins and ends. I was to learn later that every hobo carries a razor and a pocket-knife. The pocket-knife is used for shaving. Fortunately I had quite a substantial ticket of admission in the shape of my provisions, and I was welcomed, it seemed to me.

B

After a meal for which I was thankful enough, I followed the example of some of the others and lay down to get some sleep.

It was a little unfortunate that I chose as neighbour a huge, bald-headed man with a ginger stubble on his face which I later discovered had earned him the name of 'Frisco Red. He was lying on his back smoking as I lay down near him. To my practised eye he was evidently three parts boozed. He looked at me in silence, and thinking nothing more about it, I was soon asleep. Had I but known it, the whole camp was agog with anticipation. Within ten minutes I was awakened with a kick in the side which nearly stove in my ribs.

I opened my eyes to see 'Frisco Red towering over me, an ugly smile on his stubbly face. The pain of the blow was acute enough to send me staggering to my feet. In my newly acquired mood of independence I wasn't going to stand that from anyone even if this hobo was a man the size of my father.

"You dirty so-and-so," I told him and went at him with my fists. All I learned immediately was that Queensberry Rules do not obtain in hobo jungles. He caught me a kick behind the knee which doubled my legs from under me. I daresay I should have been out there and then had it not been for a couple of self-appointed referees among the onlookers who were sporting enough to hold him off until I was on my feet again. That brief respite was all I needed. I had learned the tricks of the game now, and if it was to be all-in, well, I guess I could show them some of that, too. As 'Frisco Red came at me I side-stepped and swung him the hardest upper cut I knew. He belched horribly as my fist caught him, and I can smell the whisky on his breath to-day when I think of it. The stiff bristles on his chin tore the skin from my knuckles like so much paper, but the man went down like a pole-axed ox.

I think that first fight did me more spiritual good than anything that had ever happened to me. It gave me the certainty of myself, the positive self-assurance which banished for ever the thought that I might really be the despicable wretch my father had for so long lashed with his bitter tongue. You may smile at this confession, that the mere downing of a drunken tramp should accomplish such a release of all my repressions, but I must ask you to believe it did. I was a man among men for the first time in my life. The circumstances were immaterial. I can tell you, it was a grand feeling.

In that welter of filth and whiskers, 'hooch' and bugs, I was immediately accepted as an equal — indeed a superior. I had downed 'Frisco Red. Among such men it was an enviable reputation. I won't bore you with further descriptions of my journeys from jungle to jungle. They have been adequately described lately by professional journalists and from what I have read they do not seem to have changed much in the last thirty years. But in those days, they had no news value.

III

A few months later found me in Phoenix, Arizona, and a few miles outside the city I landed my first job. That was another source of satisfaction, and my self-confidence grew in proportion. I had reached the cow-country and got a job, fulfilling my original intentions. There had, of course, been a certain amount of casual work on the way—odd jobs were for the asking in those days of labour shortage and no employer wanted a pedigree or a bunch of references—but when the foreman of the Bar T Ranch signed me on, I felt I was getting somewhere at last. It was a sizable outfit, too, with some four thousand head of cattle, I believe. But there, however, I received my first disappointment. Cow-nursing, whatever may have been written about it, I remember as very dull fare indeed. The gun-totin', hard-ridin', quick-on-the-draw, tough-as-nails *vaquero* remained to me merely something to read about. I found my companions in the bunkhouse, comparatively speaking, a very mild and companionable lot after my experiences with the gentry of the road. The romantic figure of the cowboy was replaced in my mind by that of a farm-hick on a horse. If unpleasant habits be considered tough, then at least I must say that there was little cleanliness among the men there. You wore your shirt for riding, eating, drinking and sleeping and changed it when it fell off. But out in that country—maybe the climate accounted for it—there was a general atmosphere of sleepy peace to which I didn't take kindly at all. The only time the men carried guns was when they went into town, so I guess maybe the quiet of ranch life irked them some, too, and they looked forward to a little liveliness on pay-day. The rolling, open ranges seemed to me to invite sleep, and as for the work, I have said any farm boy who can ride a horse will qualify. After I had stuck it for a time, I packed up one pay-day and made for the town. It was not Phoenix I went to this time but a small cattle-town some way south I will call Los Centrales. I was looking, if you like, for excitement, and although I did not know it at the time that can generally be translated trouble. I got it all right, but, as you will see, scarcely through any fault of my own.

One of the boys on the ranch had told me that Los Centrales, although a smaller place than Phoenix, could be reckoned on for more general entertainment. That, he said, was where some of the bad men hung around sometimes, and anyways dance halls, booze and women were all there.

That was enough for me, and to Los Centrales I went, with a pocketful of money and a large thirst. The main saloon and the general store were housed in the same building and as you rode into town you couldn't miss it. It was just across the street from the dance-hall I had heard about and resolved to visit, and as I strode in I felt that here at last I was tasting Life with money in my pocket. That feeling, however, was not to last.

I had sufficient drink to feel pleasantly communicative and it wasn't long before everyone knew that I had just come into town from the Bar T Ranch. Standing next to me at the bar was a tall, grizzled man of about forty-five wearing regulation cowboy clothes with a black sombrero. I shall not forget that face easily. After a while I heard the barman address him by his name—Thompson—and immediately I knew who he was. The boys at the ranch had often spoken of him and in fact had told me I was lucky not to be working for his outfit. He was Jed Thompson, foreman of the neighbouring ranch to Bar T, and had a reputation for being a bad-tempered bully. It did not take me long to learn that that reputation was well earned.

I daresay I may have been talking too much and too loudly in that saloon, running my mouth, as the saying is, but I was as friendly and companionable as you like. It seemed to me that my companion might care to share some of my enthusiasm and I was rash enough to turn to him and offer him a drink.

"What 'll it be, pard?" I asked him.

He turned round slowly and looked me up and down. A slightly sarcastic grin appeared on his face.

"I ain't drinkin'," he said slowly, and returned to his own tumbler of whisky.

"Sure you are," I insisted. "And with me. We're neighbours, I guess."

Jed Thompson faced me again. This time he wasn't smiling.

"Say," he said. "Didn't I tell you I ain't drinkin'? Not with —— greenhorn kids, anyways."

Those words may sound harmless enough, but in that country there is a stigma attaching to the word 'greenhorn', apart from the inference about my years, which no man will allow to pass unchallenged. Moreover, his remark was met with appreciative guffaws from a bunch of his own men with him in the saloon which only served to irritate me further. I said nothing for a moment; and then, snatching up my glass, dashed it in his face. I saw his hand go round to his gun, but for once he wasn't quite quick enough. I caught him with my doubled fist behind the ear and he staggered back. I leapt at him and caught his wrists as we fell to the floor. After that, it seemed to me, the fight became a free for all. I guess the man had a few enemies in the room, and it was not any quixotic defence of myself which prompted the mêlée which then ensued. I found myself dragged from the prostrate Thompson and lashing out in all directions. Suddenly, above the general uproar, a shot rang out. It was not from my gun, which in fact I had forgotten. I wasn't much of a shot in those days, and if it came to fighting my one idea was to get my knuckles busy. I have had good reason to know better since. However, there was a wild rush for the swing doors at the sound, and as I ran across the room I saw Jed Thompson lying where he first fell, with an ugly wound in his temple. He was unquestionably dead!

CHAPTER II

BAD MAN

I

In the mob outside a man caught my arm. "Better come with me, buddy," he said. "It won't do you no good hangin' around here with a killin' against you."

I looked at him and recognised him as a man who had been playing cards with a couple of others at one end of the saloon.

I told him to go to hell and that I was no killer anyway.

"Some guy picked a quarrel with Jed Thompson and shot him up, cowboy," he said. "Every man in that saloon will testify it was you. Better get goin', huh?"

The realisation that what he said was nothing short of the truth dawned on me with terrible suddenness. In those days sheriffs' justice did not require the evidence of ballistic experts and finger-print men. If by general consensus of opinion you were the killer of a man, why, they just hanged you and no questions asked as to how and why. It was the only sort of justice they knew.

And so it came about that I rode hard out of town with Bill Lang, outlaw, bandit, bad man. I had heard about him from the cowpokes at Bar T, but he was generally supposed to 'work' further south, toward the border. His was one of the many small-time cattle-rustling gangs operating on both sides of the Mexican border as far along as Texas, but if Bill Lang and his bunch never gained the notoriety of Jesse James and his brothers, I can promise the reader that fact does not necessarily involve his being any less unpleasant a customer. It was my first encounter with the professional bad man. Down and outs, outcasts, petty thieves—I had met them in the hobo camps. But none of them were made of the stuff that makes an expert killer.

We rode a few hours into the hills beyond Los Centrales and by nightfall had come to his hide-out. I was just the sort of man Bill Lang was looking for, and I suppose he considered that he had been lucky that day. To offer a hunted man the security of his own methods of evading the law placed me in an invidious position. It did not matter much whether he thought me guilty or not. I was an out-law in spite of myself and Bill Lang wanted extra hands. There was no question that they were look-ing for me. In a few days I was to see notices bearing my name (I had been foolish enough to mention it in the saloon) and description posted up in all small towns for many miles around!

There were seven others in the gang—all older
men than myself, and just about as hard bitten a
bunch as I had ever seen. All were Americans with
the exception of one Pedro, a Mexican or a half-
caste Spanish-Indian, who I discovered later was the
principal negotiator for the "firm" after the spoils
had been run across the border. They took kindly
enough to me and you may be sure I was not going
to protest my innocence in such company. I felt I
might as well make the best of a thorough bad job
and throw in my lot with them until a chance turned
up to allow me to pursue my own destiny again.
My principal concern at that moment was preserving
my life, and as Bill Lang anticipated, I considered
that this was the best means of doing so.

You have read enough 'westerns', I expect, not
to want a description of cattle-rustling and horse-
thieving, even an authentic one. Even the wildest
flights of fancy of the novelist cannot be far from the
truth as it was in those days. Bill Lang's enterprises
stopped at nothing. Killing, burning, everything
that was criminal, sordid, rotten. Live stock would
be run over the border into Mexico—rarely in the
same place, and there disposed of for what I daresay was a quarter of their value. The business end
of it was cut and dried. We all received a percentage
of the profits which would be spent in the same way.
Dicing, cards, women. And all the time we went in
fear of our lives. While the forces of law and order

were not very numerous, they were there, and doubly
vigilant, perhaps, because of their small numbers.
A 'wanted' man was not arrested and tried. He
was shot on sight, and if sometimes the wrong man
was shot, well, it was just too bad. Another accidental
miscarriage of justice!

And here once again I must de-bunk the atmosphere of romance which time and imagination have
woven around the old time Western gangs. There
was no Robin Hood and his Merry Men about us.
When we ventured into the towns to spend our
money, I was frequently robbed of my 'cut' by my
own companions, generally by card-cheating. But
at least I had more sense than to pick a quarrel
with them, though God knows I often felt like it.
Honour among thieves is a non-existent quantity.

It must have been about three months after I
joined up with Bill Lang that we found ourselves
one evening just outside a small village near the
town of Nogales, Arizona. New Mexico and the
western Texas border ranges had become too hot
to hold us and the idea Lang had was to ride north
and west. Pedro, the Greaser, had assured us that
he knew of an excellent source of disposal across the
Gila Desert towards Yuma and that the whole desert
country was wide-open.

We were to discover that night, however, that our
leader had other plans. Bill Lang was evidently
finding cattle-rustling a game in which the profits

did not counterbalance the risk. He had determined, therefore, on another short cut to wealth, more risky maybe, but infinitely more profitable.

At that time the stage still ran between Nogales and Arivaca—I don't think they have built the railroad through there yet—and carried passengers, mail and dust between those two points, about forty miles apart. By a little judicious enquiry in the town it seemed that Bill had ascertained the time it was expected on a certain part of the route which would be most convenient for an ambush and a quick getaway over the border. He was fortunate in possessing Pedro, who seemed to know every inch of the country along the border mountains, since the majority of us as far as I knew had never ridden that country before. According to Lang, the procedure was simple enough. Just a hold-up, he told us, and the less shootin' the better.

The next day we took up our position in a ruined adobe hut some thirty yards from the road, which gave us a commanding view in either direction. The stage was expected to pass around six o'clock that evening, and as we sat there all day drinking and smoking to pass the time, I began to feel a little jumpy. Robbery under arms was punishable with death—not always instant. In the desert country there were strange ways of executing a death sentence. . . . The torrid sun pouring down on our ruined shelter reminded me of a possible parching

thirst, and the sight of the giant cactus plants with
needle pointed leaves seemed decidedly unpleasant.
Years later I experienced the same sensations in
France, waiting to go over the top. It's the suspense
that gets a man's nerves, I guess, for Heaven knows
the thought of a little shoot-up had long ceased to
worry me.

A while before sundown we saw it. The stage
was coming along the road at a goodish pace, the
six mules throwing up a cloud of dust. At a sign
from Lang, we ran out and swung into the saddle.
We were about to ride down to the road when one
of the boys shouted: "Ain't that somethin' else thar
behind her?" He was pointing to where, a quarter
of a mile or so behind the first a *second* stage was
approaching!

I guess this had scarcely entered into Bill Lang's
calculations, for he swore volubly as he caught sight
of it. However, he was not to be deterred by mere
numbers. We had the advantage of mobility, and
the fact that the second stage was probably carrying
mail as well was, if anything, only a further inducement to carry out the hold-up.

He divided us into two parties, one for the leading
stage, the other for the one behind. I was assigned
to the first, with the Mexican, Pedro, and three
others, including Lang himself, and we were given
strict instructions to avoid shooting the mules if
possible. They were too valuable.

We rode hard down to the side of the road, and I remember a feeling of exultation at getting on the move again after the day-long wait. It simply did not occur to me then that any resistance would be offered. But I was sadly mistaken. As the first stage caught sight of us, without bothering to inquire our object, the old mule-skinner let drive. A bullet sang past my ear and I saw Lang drop from his horse. At the same time there was a fusillade from the second party. Both coaches had reined, and from the first about ten men dismounted and fired at us as we bore down on them. I heard later that the first stage was carrying no valuables and merely travelling as a convoy for the second. I guess they must have got wind of our scheme, or else somebody had tried it on that route before.

In any case, almost before we had reached the road our party numbered two—myself and the Mex. Lang and the others lay biting the dust some way back. It was a case of discretion being the better part of valour and we turned our horses and rode like hell for the hills at the foot of the Sierrieta. Inside fifty yards they got the horses under us and we ran the rest of the way.

What happened to the others I never knew. They ...st have been pretty well wiped out, except for ... son of a so-and-so who was respons... ...ce I saw some days later. ... course. Mayb...

CHAPTER II

BAD MAN

I

IN the mob outside a man caught my arm. "Better come with me, buddy," he said. "It won't do you no good hangin' around here with a killin' against you."

I looked at him and recognised him as a man who had been playing cards with a couple of others at one end of the saloon.

I told him to go to hell and that I was no killer anyway.

"Some guy picked a quarrel with Jed Thompson and shot him up, cowboy," he said. "Every man in that saloon will testify it was you. Better get goin', huh?"

The realisation that what he said was nothing short of the truth dawned on me with terrible suddenness. In those days sheriffs' justice did not require the evidence of ballistic experts and finger-print men. If by general consensus of opinion you were the killer of a man, why, they just hanged you and no questions asked as to how and why. It was the only sort of justice they knew.

man because if it hadn't been for seeing that notice I might never have headed north again. But that's the way things happen.

We were on the run all right then, I can tell you. We both knew it wouldn't be long before the sheriff's posse was out after us. We had to get going. Luck was still with us. Soon after nightfall we struck a small ranch in the foothills—corn in Egypt. What we wanted more than anything in the world was a couple of horses, and here they were right in front of us. We had to get provisioned up, too, and with this idea in mind we called in on the rancher. We had to turn 'em out of bed, I remember, an old man with his wife and daughter. We had agreed, to avoid further trouble, to buy the beasts and what-ever we took, as between us we had enough money.

It was then I had my first taste of the greaser's rotten soul. We were 'bad men' as they used to say, the pair of us, but there are some things which as long as the word 'man' is included, you just can't do. But the greaser did it that night. He didn't even start to talk about horses. He pulled his gun on the old man and shot him in the back, in fron of his wife and daughter. That got me someho and I just saw red. I killed that greaser with m hands—throttled him—praying in my heart his di soul would rot in hell. I don't want to suggest chivalrous instinct prompted me. It was

I\

wit ...ad
hea. ...at Bar T, but
he v ...to 'work' further south,
towai ...cr. His was one of the many small-time cattle-rustling gangs operating on both sides of the Mexican border as far along as Texas, but if Bill Lang and his bunch never gained the notoriety of Jesse James and his brothers, I can promise the reader that fact does not necessarily involve his being any less unpleasant a customer. It was my first encounter with the professional bad man. Down and outs, outcasts, petty thieves—I had met them in the hobo camps. But none of them were made of the stuff that makes an expert killer.

We rode a few hours into the hills beyond Los Centrales and by nightfall had come to his hide-out. I was just the sort of man Bill Lang was looking for, and I suppose he considered that he had been lucky that day. To offer a hunted man the security of his own methods of evading the law placed me in an invidious position. It did not matter much whether he thought me guilty or not. I was an out-law in spite of myself and Bill Lang wanted extra hands. There was no question that they were look-ing for me. In a few days I was to see notices bearing my name (I had been foolish enough to mention it in the saloon) and description posted up in all small towns for many miles around!

murder, deliberate and intended. But I've never regretted it.

When he lay still, I stood there hardly knowing what to say to the two women. I guess there wasn't much to be said anyway.

I buried the old man as decently as I could. The greaser was too rotten to touch. All the time the old woman was watching me. I think she must have hated me more than anything she ever saw, but she never said a thing, and I don't believe she ever put anyone on my trail. In silence she watched me take what I wanted. I took a decent *mustang* out of the corral and saddled him up. There was money enough on Pedro's body to pay for it. I filled the saddle-bag with such food as I could lay my hands on and cleared out. I was a stranger in strange country that night and that horse took me pretty well where he wanted. I figured we were still heading away from Nogales and that was good enough for me. By dawn I was nearing Tubac, about ten miles west of the Santa Cruz River.

An urgent problem had presented itself during the night. It was very apparent that dressed as I was, and mounted, I was far too conspicuous for safety. I knew they would be looking for me, and in a matter of days—or hours—a stranger can be found in that country. I had to get out of these clothes and look a little less like the night-rider I was. It dropped into my lap again. A man was walking

c

along the road beside a mule, going towards Tubac, dressed in the ordinary blue jeans and Panama of the farm hick. It was just my meat.

I reined alongside and wished him good morning. He looked up at me. I guess I may have looked rather untidy after what I had been through the day before; in any case it was evident he didn't like the looks of me because he caught the mule a welt with his whip and started to run with her. What was in his mind I don't know to this day, because it's precious little use attempting to run away, with mule, from a mounted man. I cantered ahead and dismounted. If the guy wasn't amenable to reason he'd have to be talked to some other way. All I knew was *I had to have those clothes!*

When he came up, I didn't waste time talking any more. I daresay it was hardly a fair fight, but I had to put him out. Inside five minutes I was on that mule in his jeans. I left mine beside him and turned the horse loose. I guess his pals laughed when he turned up in Tubac. I hit Santa Cruz that day and worked up toward Tucson. It was hot, too, and the going hard. It took me nearly three days to make thirty miles. I had dropped the mule early on. Muleteering was a game I had to learn later in life!

I was heartily sick of everything by then and my one idea was to get out of that country altogether. There was a railhead in Tucson and I had money in my pocket. I had to go somewhere where I could lie low for a while. There was a pretty strong public feeling about cleaning up the West at that time. It had been wide open too long. I was pretty certain they would be making an extensive search for me. I still had a killing against me and they were likely to be hunting for Bill Lang's boys who got away from the hold-up which missed fire.

As I reached Tucson I decided to take a chance and go back to Humboldt. It may sound rather odd to say I was homesick after the way I have described my departure. But there at least were people I knew, and even my old father, at that distance, did not seem to me such a tough proposition. I was pretty husky now, after what I had been through, and if he was still alive, I was pretty sure I could stand up to him if it came to it.

I went into the mail office in Tucson to send some money in advance to await me at Humboldt. I wasn't taking any chances with myself. The first thing I saw was a notice, stuck among a number of others:

Territory of Arizona

WANTED!

$250 REWARD

will be paid to the person able to give information leading to the arrest or apprehension of

DOUGLAS McHARDIE

(there followed a fairly accurate description of myself, where I was last seen and a list of my misdemeanours).

That was enough for me. It was good-bye to the Wild West and California here I come! I rode the Southern Pacific out of Tucson on the cushions and arrived in Humboldt, California within three days.

CHAPTER III

FROZEN GOLD

I

I SHALL never forget the evening of my arrival home. I had been away two years without any idea of what had happened to my parents. Until the day I had arrived in Tucson I had meant the break to be a clean one. My mind was firmly made up that I should never go back. However, my best laid plans, like those of mice and men, had ganged agley, and here I was!

I was uncertain, to say the least of it, of my reception. If it was to be a sock in the jaw I was at all events now ready to give as good as I received. But to my amazement I can only compare my home-coming to the original prodigal son's. My father received me warmly. He told me that my mother had died in my absence—to my shame, I suppose my sudden departure broke her heart—and, stranger still, I was surprised to find my reputation had preceded me. You will remember that some of the neighbours in Humboldt had sons working in the ranch country, and I suppose the news of my bad luck after leaving the Bar T had gone the rounds and someone had written home that Bob McHardie's son had become a 'bad man.'

So far from displeasing my father this news evidently convinced him that I was turning into a better man than he had once supposed. I really believe he was proud to have a fugitive, wanted for murder and robbery, as a son. At any rate, after telling me I was a blockheaded fool and would probably end on the gallows where I belonged, he remarked:

"Ye'd better stick quietly around for a while, Dougal, boy, until the trouble blows over. I'll see they don't get to know ye're here."

And so for a month I hid up, never going out, avoiding the eyes of the neighbours, until one night my father came to my room and asked me what I was going to do. I agreed with him that it was useless staying in Humboldt like this indefinitely, but confessed that my mind was not particularly fertile with ideas for the future.

Over a bottle of whisky my father made my mind up for me. The decision I took involved a complete get-away and the chance of making a mint of money. GOLD!

It was a bare two years since the famous rush of '98 to the Klondyke, and tales still came through regularly of fabulous strikes, which sent thousands to the North every year.

It was a suggestion which suited me admirably. "But how in hell," I inquired of my father, "do you think I'm going to get there? I never did go much for walking, and I guess I've had enough of it anyway."

The reply was certainly a shock to accepted ideas.

"I'm going to give ye some money, Dougal," said the old man, and to my utter amazement he handed me four hundred dollars! With what I already possessed, this sum would see me there in comparative comfort, and I thanked him warmly.

"Ye don't deserve it, boy," he said, "but ye're an awfu' responsibility around this city."

I really believe that had it not been for my untimely return my father intended to go North himself. What strange dormant streak of paternal affection prevented him, I have never explained to myself, for I swear that was the one and only kindness I ever received from him. I mention the possibility of his own intention to go prospecting because he seemed already equipped with all the information as to how to get there and what points to make for. I was to go to Seattle, it seemed, and take the boat there to Skagway. From there to Dawson City, from which the prospectors set out for the creeks, was about 600 miles along the trail. Properly equipped, you should make it in three or four days along the trail.

The day I left Humboldt for Seattle my father was drunk. I never said good-bye to him, and I

heard later that within a short time of my departure
he was killed in a saloon fight. I cursed the man
who killed him, not for any sentimental reason, but
because he took away my opportunity to fulfil the
kid's oath that one day I would better the old man
in every direction.

The boat which took me from Seattle to Skagway
upset my notions considerably. Not unnaturally I
had a vague idea that anybody who proposed to
make a few years' stay in the 'Frozen North' would
have taken some steps to assure himself that he was
the type of man to stand the climate and conditions.
It was common knowledge that living up there was
tough and the temperature so low it didn't deserve
the name. But I was mistaken about my fellow-
prospectors. That boat, and I suppose all the others
that ever made the voyage, was filled with every sort
of man God ever made and a lot He didn't. The
only thing they had in common was the one motivat-
ing idea—*Gold!* What a bunch! There were store
clerks, salesmen, old sourdoughs, hoboes, sailors,
engineers, negroes, everything that ever walked or
crawled from the ends of the earth. Wops, Bohunks,
Spicks, Britishers, Chinks and the rest. And the
professional gamblers. They were the wise guys,
those sharks. It took me a long time to discover
that they—and the women—were the only ones who
ever brought a fortune out of the Klondyke. You'll
realise why I say that, later.

I remember little enough of the voyage except for the last hundred miles to Skagway. The boats used to take the Inner Passage via Katchekan which brought you through the Chatham Strait into what they called the Lynn Canal. That was a sight! Imagine a sort of fjiord, a hundred miles long and about five wide, the cliffs on either side rising three to four thousand feet. It's like sailing through a gigantic cañon. I had little enough time and patience to waste on the beauties of nature but you couldn't help noticing that. When I think of the cold white hell which lies beyond, it seems kind of odd to find it so lovely there.

The following year we heard one of the out-going boats was wrecked in this passage, just out of Skagway. She was taking back quite a crowd of folks who'd made enough and had the sense to get out of the Klondyke. The boat holed up on a rock and started to go down right away. The skipper gave orders to abandon ship, but not one of those passengers would leave her with all that gold aboard. So she lies there now, ship, crew, passengers and gold, an object lesson in greed. I don't believe a man was saved.

On the boat I made a pal. It was the first fellow-man I had ever felt an *instinctive* friendship for, and he seemed to feel the same way about me. He was a great ox of a man, a Swede named Hansen, standing about six foot four in his socks and made in

proportion. He was a great guy, that Swede. In
the months that followed before we made Dawson
City I often tried to pick a quarrel with him out
of sheer devilment, but he'd never take a hazing
from me. More than once I saw Hansen drop a
man to the floor with as little effort as pressing a
button, and I guess he could have broken my back,
tough as I was, with one arm. But he never gave
me a chance to discover. All I could get him to
say was: "You are yust fool, Mac." And he'd laugh
at my efforts to get a rise out of him. And could
that man drink? I thought my old man was a good
hand, but Hansen could have drunk him under and
then enough to drown him in a bath.

It is difficult to imagine without having seen it
the picture that Skagway presented in the year 1900.
It was a collection of log shacks with a resident
population of perhaps a few hundreds. Day after
day boatloads of humanity—there's no other word—
were unshipped and dumped there. They had
arrived in Alaska! Many who came appeared to
believe that handfuls of precious gold were there
for the picking up. They had rushed precipitately
to the nearest point without the remotest conception
of what tremendous difficulties, what hardships confronted even the most determined man before he
reached the Klondyke creeks. They came in their
thousands, unprepared, inappropriately clothed, some
even penniless on their arrival. It was sheer madness,

and as might be expected, the death-rate even in Skagway itself was enormous. How many lives petered out along the trail scarcely bears thinking about. It was a Trail of Death, paved with greed!

The pair of us hung around in Skagway, as you might expect, until we were both flat broke. The Klondyke seemed such a long way off, we must have figured we might as well have a good time before we started trying to get there. But the time came in a few weeks when we began to think about getting on the trail. During our stay in Skagway one thing had struck me pretty forcibly, and that was the fact that hundreds came off the boats and never got any further than the first saloon because they were too soft even to make the first fifty miles out of Skagway up to the top of the Chilkoot, 3,000 feet above, which was the gateway to the Klondyke and the Upper Yukon mining country. They couldn't even get themselves up there, far less carry their trappings. As for getting on to the trail after that——! There was no organised transport system then. A man just had to get there somehow, and we were prepared to help them if they were prepared to pay. It was an idea which worked. Hansen and I were both man-size, and the weedy clerks who got bogged in Skagway were willing to pay plenty for our services. The scheme was, of course, to furnish ourselves with sufficient capital to equip our own expedition properly, as we reckoned by that time we should know exactly what we wanted to get us through with a fair amount of certainty instead, as so many did, of rushing along the trail, badly equipped, unprovisioned, and dying of hunger or exposure along the trail. The Yukon and White Pass Railroad, which makes it easy for any tourist to get to the Klondyke nowadays, had yet to be built. In those days you mushed it with a dog-sled.

Hansen thought it was a swell scheme, as he was keener even than I was to get up to Dawson as soon as possible. Accordingly, after we had examined the route from Skagway to Summit—the frontier station at the top of the Chilkoot, beyond which lay Yukon Territory—we started in the porterage business! Anyone we saw we told that we were willing, for a substantial consideration, to tote kit and provisions up to Summit and set them on the long 465 mile trail to Dawson.

We didn't have to look for business! We had more than we could cope with and as we could ask pretty well what we liked we found it comfortably profitable. A man would pay almost anything just to get there, so certain was he that El Dorado lay at the other end of the trail. What terrible disillusionment awaited most of them!

Hansen and I worked this game for months, eventually enlisting the services of two other men, one a Scotsman named Forbes, the other an Italian whose name I've forgotten. They were both tough, husky fellows, and when eventually the time came, we all decided to throw in our lot together and make Dawson in a party of four. We reckoned there was more likelihood of us getting through that way, I suppose on the principle of safety in numbers.

II

During the time we were in the porterage business we had been busy collecting all the information we could about the surest way of reaching the Yukon. The journey had to be made early in the year if you wanted to use dog-sleds, since after April the trail was mushy. The only other way after that time until the winter was to take a boat down the river, through Lake Lebarge on to the Lewes River to where it joins the Yukon at Stewart and so on to Dawson. The principal difficulty about this route, although it meant saving of time, was its extreme danger. I don't suppose one man in ten got through that way. To begin with, in the spring the water was full of floating ice, and at the very outset you had to shoot the White Horse rapids. Take a look at them, reader, if you ever chance that way as a comfortable tourist. I think you will agree it's a very uncertain gamble with a nasty death.

However, Hansen was all for chancing it. If we didn't go that way, he argued, it meant months of waiting for the trail to harden, and what was more, the boat wasn't built that he couldn't handle. I guess these Swedes are born to it in their own country.

"But the boat isn't built, anyway," I told him.

"We're going to build it," he said. Out of the proceeds of our carrying business it appeared that Hansen had purchased timber and tools and proposed to tote them up to Summit and build the boat there to shoot the rapids down to White Horse. He was pretty handy as a carpenter and if keenness counted for anything, then we three others could be reckoned on for plenty of assistance. So we agreed to take a chance on it.

It took us quite a few days to provision up. There was one staple and unvarying diet for the man heading North in those days. Bacon or sow's belly, beans and plenty of flour. That went for the dogs, too, if you took the trail. They didn't feed huskies with dried fish along that route!

I don't know anything about the dietetic properties of this grub, but I can guarantee it to hold a man's soul in his body longer than anything else up there in the Cold Country.

We made Summit at the end of the fifty-six mile climb out of Skagway on the second day, and the first thing we heard when we got up there was the grim news that two men had overturned in White Horse rapids the week before. If you look at that rushing inferno of foaming white water with its treacherous needle pointed rocks beneath you'll wonder, as I did, how anything can stand up to it for five minutes, much less make the fifty odd miles to White Horse. The idea that we should try seemed crazy to me and I said so.

Forbes and the Wop must have felt more careless or more desperate, for it was their unvarnished hints that I was possessed of a yellow streak which made me change my mind. After all, I had precious little to lose. . . .

We built the boat there—a good stout workmanlike affair; no flimsy canoe would take the beating we were going to get. And then, at midday on a Friday we took the water on the start of our long trip to Dawson. There wasn't anything like an even chance that we should make it, but we shot those rapids, four men, baggage and provisions and came ashore at White Horse just after sundown!

The 'town' of White Horse, at the mouth of the strip of river known as the Thirty-Mile, beyond which lies Lake Lebarge, was just a few shacks then, but there must have been a hundred men there, mostly sleeping under canvas, waiting till the ice was out of the river. The only form of amusement provided was betting on the exact hour and day that this would occur!

We only stayed there long enough to cut spruce from the surrounding forests and make a serviceable sled, and we picked up one husky—just in case. We found him pretty useful later.

The next day we made the Thirty-Mile and went ashore at night at the mouth of the lake. The next morning we awoke to find we were presented with a distinctly unpleasant job. The annual thaw had only just set in—it was early April—and the whole surface of the lake was still practically covered with ice, although the river was flowing underneath. This made the ice crack and shift ceaselessly while the edge of the lake was a mass of moving floes. It was hopeless to progress further by boat, and we determined to take to the sled for as much of the fifty mile length of Lebarge as we could. It took us nearly two hours to get on to the ice and within a couple of miles the sled overturned! The ice was treacherously thin in parts and our efforts to right the sled and get ashore again resulted in more than one icy ducking. A man doesn't stay in water at that temperature for more than five minutes and live. We worked feverishly to get ashore and thaw out before a fire before we froze to death. We made it in the end, but the following day the Italian took sick. This meant that we were carrying a deadweight in addition to losing one man, and didn't make matters any easier. It was very slow going along the rest of Lake Lebarge. The main ice was far enough from the bank at times to allow us to put the loaded boat in the water, while we walked along the lakeside and the husky dragged her. Every night we turned in completely exhausted, after repeatedly hauling the boat ashore all day to prevent her being crushed by the ice as it moved toward the bank. Great herds of caribou used to come and watch us sometimes, thousands of them, but we had no gun and were obliged to tolerate them as unwelcome spectators.

At last we reached the end of the lake and took to the water again. The ice was out, and the rest of the journey could be made in the boat. The journey grew terribly monotonous. Very occasionally we would pass some other prospectors on the bank, but for the most part we just pulled unceasingly over the crystal clear river. (It is so transparent that the river bed many feet below is easily visible!)

At last we approached the final obstacle. We had been told at White Horse that we might get down the Yukon River but we should never pass the dreaded Five Fingers! These are five needle pointed rocks standing up sheer out of the middle of the river and setting up eddies and cross-currents which were reputed to drag the boats and dash them against the rock. Only Hansen's magnificent handling of the boat got us through. It was his turn at the steering oar in the stern and if it were not for him, we should never have got through. But we did, and our goal was in sight. The only remaining difficulty was negotiating the mouth of the Klondyke where it meets the Lewes and creates a tremendous cross-current which is quite capable of carrying a boat two miles beyond Dawson with the prospect of

D

getting back upstream. That patch was the worst
pull of the lot, especially as we were almost all in
already. But on the Sunday week following the Friday
we had started we stood on the river bank at Dawson
City and breathed the heartiest sigh of relief we'd
ever draw. We could count ourselves among the few
who had beaten the river and we felt pretty pleased
with ourselves. The first place we made for was the
nearest saloon, and that evening the Wop made a
surprising recovery after being sick all the trip!
I've never thought much of Italians since. . . .

CHAPTER IV

I BECOME A SOURDOUGH

I

Dawson? In appearance it was just like any other mining camp in the earlies. It was a city in name only. Jack London has put it on the literary map, with the aid of his fertile imagination. I told him so years later, when I met him in San Francisco. That was a laugh, too. But I'm getting too far ahead.

The principal point I want to make about the accepted idea of Dawson City in the gold rush days and Dawson as it actually was, is the comparatively peaceful community I found there. Gaston the half-breed, wolf dogs, bad men, shoot-ups, in fact all the usual accompaniments of stories of the Frozen North simply weren't there.

It was rough and ready to be sure, and there were certain undesirable characters—there are in every collection of human beings—but as for shooting, I never saw a gun fired in six years.

I only ever heard of one killing and that was up in the Chilkoot. Some *cheechako*[1] had his baggage pinched at the mouth of the White Horse and cut

[1] The Indian word for greenhorn generally in use among the prospectors.

up rough about it. It didn't take the Mounties long to find their man that time! The atmosphere of glamour which time and fiction-writers have built round this force is another idol I should like to shatter. They never have a thing to do up there except act as stool-pigeons for the municipal police! And the last time I was in Canada, the appearance of a "Mountie" was the signal for a shower of stones and shouts of derision from the children. I think the old-timers bagged a few Indians for killing when the force first formed but I don't believe they've got three white men on their homicide list. Most of their time was spent arresting claim-jumpers.

The only 'bad man' in the North died a year or so before my arrival. It was the notorious Soapy Smith, whose grave, inscribed with the only name by which he was known, stands on a hill outside Skagway. He and a bunch of other men used to hold up sleds along the trail and rob them of what they were carrying. I don't think he used much violence, either, but his unfortunate victims were often starved before reaching civilisation. There was precious little crime of any sort after his demise.

Men were too busy trying to make fortunes in the creeks and losing them at the tables. Generally speaking I don't believe I ever met a better collection of men than the crowd up in the Yukon in those years. I guess you had to have a pretty good streak in you to get there, even. You could always find someone to help you if you were really down. It's big, the country up there, really big, and a man had to be big in every way to get by.

There was a sort of open-handed, *communal* atmosphere about the whole of that collection of log shacks they called a city, which I never experienced anywhere else. I believe there was a good deal of unrestricted crime in the placer mining camps of the Western United States, but up in the Yukon we were a peaceable crowd. Maybe the climate or the environment has something to do with it, but anyway it is a fact which any old sourdough will corroborate.

When I said that only a few prospectors ever brought fortunes back from the North I did not mean to infer that gold was not there. It was, and plenty of it. The first year I was up in the creeks (1900) gold was panned in the Yukon totalling $22,000,000. There was gold there right enough. But the difficulty was to get it out of the country. What can you expect a man to do after working in arctic conditions, often entirely alone, for eight or nine months? He gets to the nearest point which approaches civilisation and spends his earnings. In that case it meant Dawson City. The money went to the professional gamblers, the saloon keepers and the women.

II

After our journey from Skagway I felt like a couple of weeks' rest, I can tell you, and nothing

was going to stop me taking it. Hansen and the
others couldn't wait. They were crazy to get up
to the creeks to get their hands on some dust, like a
good many more, I guess. So we parted company
the day after our arrival. They pulled out of Dawson,
and I stopped around to have a look at the town. I
only saw them once or twice, quite casually, after
that. Our ways lay in different directions.

My intended fortnight lengthened into three weeks,
then a month, until I found myself once more without
resources, this time within a couple of hundred
miles of the Arctic Circle. You might imagine I
must have been living pretty fast to spend my entire
capital in a month, as I arrived with well-lined
pockets after our successful enterprise in Skagway.
However, beyond getting drunk occasionally and
taking a hand at poker once in a while I could scarcely
reproach myself with high living. The ordinary
expenses of existence were fantastically high. You
had to be half a millionaire to keep yourself in the
bare necessities of life in Dawson. Eggs of dubious
age rated $1½ apiece, flour was $10 per stone, bacon
a dollar a pound, whisky $10 a bottle, while the
luxury of a shave would cost you two dollars and a
half! Most of us were economically be-whiskered in
consequence.

You will see, then, that you just had to have money
or die, which was as much accountable for the
immense productivity in the creeks as the idea that

anyone was going to make a fortune and retire to civilisation.

I was beginning to feel a little concerned about the cost of my 'holiday', as at the end of four weeks I had exactly twenty dollars left and not much idea of how I was going to earn enough to get myself out to the creeks for a nine months' stop-over. I was sitting in one of the saloons one evening watching the play at the tables and I suppose I must have looked pretty disconsolate because an oldish man standing beside me said: "You ain't playin' then, son?"

I told him I couldn't even if I wanted to.

He grinned sympathetically. "I guess you ain't been here long, *cheechako*," he said. "Kind of fresh to it, huh?"

I agreed.

"I came out here in the first boat load in '96," he informed me, "and by the time I made Dawson I didn't have two red cents. How much you got left?" he asked suddenly.

I told him. "Twenty dollars."

"Do you want to make a livin' fer a time? I ain't promisin' a fortune, but some nights you may strike lucky."

"Sure," I said. "Anything to keep going for a while."

"Well," he growled, "you kin be swamper right here fer ten dollars a week, and I guess you ought to clear thirty. The feller who's bin doin' it is leavin' town to-night."

"What's a swamper?" I asked him.

"Cleanin' up the floors an' tables. I shan't ask you but ten dollars a week for the privilege."

It was the first time I realised that I was to *pay* for this work! The old man, it seemed, kept the saloon and the price he named entitled me to the sole rights of panning the water used for swabbing the premises for gold dust! In the case of prospectors returning from the creeks it was quite customary to accept dust instead of coin for any purchases in the stores and saloons. Every saloon-owner had his scales mounted on the bar and the same prices were given there for dust as at the banks. Of course, a certain amount was lost in handling and it was generally reckoned that the floor sweepings and swabbings would show a 'swamper' a decent weekly profit while ensuring a cleaning service to the saloon-keeper for which he was *paid!*

I took the job on his word, and sure enough at the end of the first week found it was showing me a very handsome return. (When I was back in Dawson in 1925, by a strange chance they were just pulling down that old saloon I worked in, and I heard from the wreckers that they had panned nearly a hundred dollars worth of gold from under the floor boards!)

By now I was getting anxious myself to get out to the creeks, and I used to take a chance on the tables at the end of each week with my 'swamping' profits. A run of luck for a few consecutive weeks put me on my feet once more and I was at last able to buy an outfit and get out to stake a claim.

The wildest rumours used to circulate in Dawson every time a bunch came in from the creeks about rich strikes and entirely fabulous lodes. There was a good deal of practical joking as a result and one incident which I remember well is worth relating.

A crowd was standing at the bar one night in the saloon where I worked when a young man came in who had evidently just returned from a prospecting trip. There were the usual excited queries as to how he had fared and after demurring for some time he produced a darkish lump of rock from a bag and handed it round. It bore a number of vari-coloured markings and there was a good deal of speculation as to whether it was gold-bearing or not. No one could say for certain, and eventually the expert services of an old sourdough of a prospector were requisitioned to give a definite decision. He examined it carefully under the light and eventually delivered his judgment in the form of a highly technical list of geological terms, which he stated, was the composition of the rock. Everyone waited breathlessly until at last he pronounced that it certainly did possess quite a high percentage of gold!

The owner then spoke.

"Dad," he said, "I believe you're wrong."

The old man instantly bridled. "There ain't a man in the Klondyke," he said, "knows more about gold-bearing formations than me, and you kin ask who you like."

"Will you take a bet?" asked the owner of the mystery.

"Sure I'll take a bet," shouted the old sourdough, banging his fist on the bar. "A bottle of rye if I'm wrong."

The young man nodded. "Done," he said. Then turning to the company announced solemnly: "This, gentlemen, is nothing more nor less than a lump of *frozen haggis!*"

And it was.

Another false alarm which started a sudden rush to the creeks was once when old Sitka Charlie, an Indian guide well known in Dawson City at the time, came into one of the stores with a lump of gold-bearing rock. This time there was no question about it; there was gold in it. Indians were not allowed to stake claims for themselves at that time, but Sitka Charlie was no fool. He volunteered to take any man who would pay $50 to the place where he had picked it up, *on the surface!* The word went round like wildfire: "Charlie's found the mother-lode," and there was a scramble to give him his $50—he must have cleared $5,000 that night. When he led them to the place, not another thing was found. The Indian may have been perfectly honest and picked up some lump which had drifted down from perhaps a hundred miles away. These lumps, known as 'drift' were quite frequently found without any relation to their surroundings.

Anyway, as I said, I went up to the creeks which lay about 20 miles from Dawson and pegged a claim. From certain remarks dropped (which, I must confess, were not meant for my ears!) while I was swamping I was fairly certain I should find something.

As was fairly usual, for reasons I will state later, I had a partner. He was a fellow from the eastern states by the name of Hollins, and whatever brought him out there I never discovered, but I guess he was the black sheep of the family from the way he spoke. He was a taciturn sort of man, well-educated, from his speech, and when I found him he was down on his luck. Some of the fellows would hire a man to go up with them for the winter to help pan and get the stuff to the top, and he was looking for a job of that sort.

With my limited resources I couldn't afford that, especially as I had no guarantee that I'd find at all, so I suggested he should come on a percentage of takings, if any. We struck a bargain, and after I had registered my claim in Dawson, we went back to the creek.

Within two weeks of our arrival we struck! It was impossible to know how much we were going to get out, but the little we managed to pan while

working raised our hopes considerably. Getting
the gold in those days was no joke. It's all pan-
mining out there, as there never has been a lode
discovered in the Yukon and I don't suppose there
ever will be. For the last few thousand years it has
been gradually dispersing. There were no machine-
worked dredges and everything had to be done by
hand. In the first place we had to get through twenty
or thirty feet of glacier ice to sink our "shaft",
and that meant melting it with boiling water. It
took twenty years for the folks up there to discover
that cold water would melt ice just as well. We
worked all through the winter at a temperature of
40 below—and sometimes colder than that—one of
us down the shaft with a pick and shovel, piling earth
and bedrock into a bucket which the other man would
haul up by hand-winch to the surface and lower
again.

Now you can understand why I needed a partner.
Added to the difficulty and discomfort of working we
had to wait until the spring before we could do any
panning or washing to see whether our efforts had
been worth while.

There was a happy ending to that first expedition,
and we got back to Dawson with about 3,000 dollars
worth of pay-dirt. After sinking a certain amount
of this in a new outfit for next season, I proceeded,
quite deliberately, to blue the rest!

I had a good time that summer, although it doesn't

sound very attractive written down. Booze, dice,
cards, women. Raw, I suppose, but after six months
of that hell, very welcome.

Women were pretty scarce in Dawson. The few
who were there had come for one purpose—to make
money. No man was crazy enough to bring his wife.
A few of the prospectors had taken Indian or Eskimo
women. Squaw-men, we called them, and they didn't
rate very high socially. Even out there, in that
rabble of tough, hard-bitten sourdoughs, there were
fairly rigid notions of what a white man could and
could not do.

Not that the standards of moral behaviour towards
the white women was especially high. It could
hardly be expected, since these were almost without
exception ladies of easy virtue. No right-minded
woman would ever go up to Dawson City for her
health. They were the original gold-diggers, those
dames. On one of my trips up to the creeks I felt
like a little companionship and I was prepared to pay
handsomely for it. I didn't think, though, that I
should be the hero of one of the tales that are told
to this day in Dawson City. It came about this way.

I had taken a fancy to a little French girl who
was up there, and after a while I suggested she might
like to accompany me on my next prospecting trip.
We had a little palaver and eventually she agreed to
come—on her own terms. I got a shock when I
heard them, but being young and foolish, I paid.

She asked that she should be put on the scales in one of the stores—the type they used for weighing flour-bags. The other side of the balance had to be filled with gold-dust until the scales were even! It was the first and last time I ever saw a woman who was worth her weight in gold. It came to about $5,000. That may sound a little odd, but as I said, women were scarce in Dawson at that date, and like other commodities, they fetched high prices. Moreover, if you don't believe it, my friend Jack Doyle who still keeps the "Principal" saloon in Dawson can corroborate me.

III

The prospecting game lasted me for six years, and at the end of that time I guess I'd had about enough. I'd gained a lot, lost a lot and, above all, learned a lot. But, as they say, I was born with itching feet. I figured that any trouble there might have been connected with my name down South would have blown over by then. In any case, the description they issued of me at the time of the Arizona hold-up wouldn't have tallied. From just a husky kid I was something like a man now. Those years in the Yukon had made me tough. I could feel I was good and hard and the aptitude for a good scrap which I must have inherited from my father had proved to me plenty of times that I was also hard to beat. I think I went about 210 pounds when I left Dawson, and not much of that was soft or flabby.

I felt I wanted to get back in the sun. California was in my mind again as it was to be once more in my life, years after. I wasn't going to make my home in Dawson like some of the fellows who went up north at the same time as myself and are still there. I met some old pals when I went back in 1925, and asked one what he found about that hellhole that was so darned attractive he had to spend all his life there. He looked at me for a moment and his wrinkled face broke into a smile. "Buddy," he said, "can you find me a job outside the Yukon where I can work four months in the year and earn enough to keep myself in grub and a little enjoyment for the rest of it? You know you can live comfortable here now on a hundred dollars a month. Besides," he added, "maybe there'll be a rich strike again one day and when it comes, I'm right here, on the spot, boy."

And that, I suppose is the spirit that keeps men there for a lifetime, hoping that perhaps to-morrow— or the day after. . . .

Do you wonder I called the North the Land of Disappointed Men?

CHAPTER V

I

I CLEARED out of Dawson one fine spring morning
with ten thousand dollars in my pocket, and I can
tell you I took the trail in style that time. They
were already operating stern-wheel paddle boats
from Dawson to White Horse and that was the way
I got back. I smiled as I remembered my arrival
and wondered if Hansen and Forbes and the Wop
had fared as well as myself.

Back in Seattle, I took the train down to San
Francisco, where I had never been, although it was
not very far from Eureka and Humboldt.

It was just after the great 'quake that I arrived
in the city and everywhere were scenes of feverish
rebuilding activity. I was pretty anxious not to
repeat my experiences in Dawson—of being broke
after a prolonged and liquid 'holiday', and after I
had taken a look around I made up my mind to
invest the major part of my capital in a business.

There was only one business at that date that I
knew much about and what I had learnt had been

on the wrong side of the bar. I had seen enough, however, to persuade me that saloon-keeping was a profitable game, particularly if you were not too fastidious about the type of customer you entertained. There was one spot in 'Frisco where I figured a saloon-keeper was bound to make money; that was along the notorious Barbary Coast (which had been spared by the 'quake and at that date had not been 'cleaned up' by the authorities). Accordingly, for the sum of 5,000 dollars I purchased lock, stock and barrel, as a going concern, "The Thousand Delights Saloon" on Kearney Street. (This street itself was known among seafaring men, for a number of reasons, as "The Street of a Thousand Delights" and I suppose it was from that that my house derived its picturesque name!)

It was one of the biggest saloons on the waterfront section with a long bar, plenty of mirrors and a dance-hall at the rear end. I had about nine gaming tables in play there as well; faro, poker, roulette and anything which brought the money in, and I ran the place high, wide and open. The sky was the limit and I never shut down from year's end to year's end. My liquor was the cheapest in town —I saw to that—and it wasn't long before the guy I bought it off was kicking himself for letting me have it so cheap. It was scarcely a place for Sunday-school treats, of course, and every man behind the bar had to qualify for the job with his fists. I think

E

at one time I had seven ex-pugs with me to keep the peace—or something like it, but they were all good boys and as loyal as they come. Drunken sailors are a tough proposition sometimes, and I needed all I could get to carry on a legitimate business for those who came in for a quiet game at the tables. Saloon-keeping thirty years ago on the old Barbary Coast was no baby's work. To begin with I soon found I had to square the police. Even there I was in competition with my neighbours. But the money rolled in and it wasn't long before I had the best custom in Kearney Street.

I used to get all sorts of people in that joint. One of the regulars was a writer named Jack London, the man who put the Frozen North into everyone's homes, and who knew exactly as much about it as can be gathered on a couple of tourist trips from Seattle. I used to haze the life out of him about it, and he wasn't always so even-tempered after my chaff. He was a short, stocky little man, with a very loud mouth, and not infrequently three-parts drunk on arrival in "The Thousand Delights." He was very sensitive about his books, particularly as every word he wrote was sheer agony. The only schooling he ever had was a few months at night-school, and while he knew what he wanted to write, it was a tremendous labour for him to get it down. I believe it was that which drove him to drink so heavily. I heard while I was there that he wrote

every word of "John Barleycorn" while he had the
horrors! But like a lot of little men he was full of
bounce, and more than once we had to bounce him
out, Jack London or no.

Another of our regular customers was the man
who discovered gold in Nome, Alaska. I've forgotten
his name but I remember him telling me he was a
journeyman tailor. He'd been shanghaied out of one
of the water-front saloons down by the Embarcadero
somewhere, some years back, and found himself
heading north on board some whaling supply ship.
He didn't care for sailoring much, and he and another
fellow determined to jump the ship just as soon as
the chance occurred. They didn't get away until
she was lying off Cape Nome, toward the Bering
Strait. Then they sneaked off one night in one of
the ship's boats, beached her, and walked a few
miles along the foreshore. Before they had quite
realised what they were doing, they were walking
on—GOLD! The sandy beach contained the only
surface-gold ever found in such circumstances, and
in July, 1899, they started digging in earnest. The
journeyman-tailor was one of the few men who had
the sense to clean up and get out, for by the time
I saw him in my saloon he was reputed to be a
multi-millionaire.

II

I don't propose to whitewash my activities at that time. Money had put ideas into my head and I soon had a finger in every racket in 'Frisco except dope and women. I will say I never went for those games. Doss-houses, crimp-houses, every kind of racket but that. Of course, the ladies of the town frequented "The Thousand Delights". In Rome you have to act Roman. But they went about their own business without interfering with mine, and as a matter of fact they stimulated custom. I can only write the facts as I saw them, and leave it to better men to moralise on the rights and wrongs of it all.

When I took over the saloon it was mostly men who ran the tables. It seemed the best thing to me, as where there are women in a business there is generally trouble as well. There was, however, one girl there, running a faro table, and when I arrived as boss I made up my mind she must go. She was a tall creature, dark-haired but with a very white skin, a mixture of German and Spanish blood, and her name was Inez. I don't believe she had any other. She was pretty popular with the boys who came in, although there was no nonsense about her and I reckon she had the ability to cuss as well as any sailor who ever played at her table.

Nevertheless, in my opinion, she was out of place. I wanted nothing but men running that joint and I told her so a few days after I took over.

"I'm sorry, sister," I said, "to make it appear like putting you out, but this is a man's job to my way of thinking, and that's the way I figure to run it. You can take a double pay-check and skip— to-night!"

She looked at me very old-fashioned for a moment before answering. I couldn't help laughing, because I believe she thought I was afraid of her.

"Oh," she said, tossing her head. "So it's that way?" (She spoke with a sort of accent I can't get on to paper.) "The new boss, huh? Well, just listen to this, big Mac. I've been running this table for quite a while and what is more I shall be running it for quite a while. In fact, just as long as I care to soil my hands in this dirty lowdown joint, and you can get right to hell and stay there!"

The look in her eye told me she meant what she said. It was a little awkward. I had scarcely expected this, after the monetary inducement. However, I had meant what I said, too. She just had to go.

"You'll leave here," I told her, "and to-night, even if I have to throw you out, lady. Bob!" I called to one of the helps behind the bar. "Bring me fifty bucks." As I turned round to her again, I had the shock of my life. Women wore long skirts in those days, and plenty of them, yet from somewhere, quicker than lightning, she yanked out a knife and made a dive at me. I did a side-step, but not quick enough to miss a nasty slash on my hand. I've got the scar to this day.

I had to laugh again, then. "All right, Inez," I said, "I guess you can stay right here. Forget I ever said anything."

She had her points, that woman, as well as spirit, because there and then she took my arm and ordered up a bottle of rye which we drank together while she bandaged my hand.

That may sound a rather odd beginning to a romance, and I don't know whether it deserves that name, but anyway after that I began to look at her in another light from just an employee. As you have probably gathered I had never had much opportunity, apart from use, for women, and when I reached 'Frisco nothing was further from my mind than that I should ever want any woman to marry me. However, I was making out pretty well in "The Thousand Delights" and after I formed this attachment for Inez, the idea of settling down to the good things of life seemed distinctly attractive. I was young enough then to have ambition, and I guess the climate suited me. There was one other thing which had lately occupied my thoughts, too, which may also seem a little strange, although if you

remember my own upbringing perhaps it was under-
standable. I wanted a son of my own. I wanted a
kid I could give a decent chance to, something I
could make an absolute contrast to all the childish
hell I went through up in Humboldt. It was an
idea which, now that I was handling real money, I
could not escape, and the opportunity of realising
it in Inez seemed to present itself very suitably. I
must ask the reader not to misjudge me for selecting
that girl as a likely wife. She was good, in spite of
the perhaps unpleasant picture of her I have given
you. You must remember the social stratum in
which I was moving. It was the only one I knew,
and you can take it from me it isn't such a bad one
at that. The ugly side of human nature is more
apparent, I suppose, and that is all the difference
between those people and any others that I ever
found.

After a while I asked Inez to marry me. I pointed
out the comparative security of my position, and it
was a fact that we got on very well. I told her also
that I wanted a son. She was very understanding
and sympathetic and listened patiently while I out-
lined my plans for the future. At the end of it all
she took my hand and said quite simply: "Mac, I
appreciate the compliment, but I'm not the marrying
sort. I just don't get there. I like you enough, sure
but well—I just can't get tied even to the best man
on earth."

So we left it like that. I had my son just the same, but not for long. Within three years I left 'Frisco for good and never saw him again. He died when he was thirteen. I believe, in spite of everything, I was glad when I heard that. I never had the chance to carry out my intentions. . . .

My profits from the saloon went from strength to strength and at last the day came when I was beginning to have my fingers in sufficient pies to arouse the attention of the less scrupulous type of American politician. I received a covert suggestion one night from a certain influential man that I might care to enter politics myself. There was, he told me, room for a young man of my ability (and I suppose he meant lack of scruple). I began to get interested and conjured up visions of myself, frock-coated and silk-hatted with a pile of gold in twenty banks.

These pipe dreams, however, soon came to a sudden and tragic conclusion. I didn't know where I was burning my fingers!

To this day I have never discovered who was the cause of my unexpected departure from America. It may perhaps have been one of my competitors in Kearney Street who considered I was getting too big for my boots. It may, on the other hand, have been the result of my beginning to dabble in politics. It may (although I have never brought myself to consider this seriously) have been Inez herself. There is no accounting for the minds of women.

They resemble the Almighty in the one respect that they move in a mysterious way. But whatever the cause, I woke up one morning with a head the size of the dome of the Capitol and a mouth like the Sahara, in the foul-smelling fo'c'sle of a boat on the high seas. *I had been shanghaied!*

CHAPTER VI

BEFORE THE MAST

I

WHEN I said I awoke, I should perhaps have written that I was brought to. An exceptionally sour-faced giant was standing over me, prepared to empty the remaining contents of the bucket of bilgewater which had already revived me so successfully. There were three of us lying together.

"Get up you lousy so-and-sos," he growled at us. "There's no time aboard this hooker to lie sleepin' all day. Get down to the galley and find some grub, then report to me."

As a parting sign of his authority he selected me for a vicious kick in the ribs which sent a pain like a knife-thrust darting through my head. I picked myself up with some difficulty and tried to remember what had happened. I had been taking a few drinks with a party of customers—I believe their faces were familiar—the night before, when—I didn't remember what happened after that. They had got me out the only way they could, I supposed. Doped the drink! I felt pretty mad about that.

I knew this practice still existed where a skipper was short of hands just before sailing; as a matter of fact, I had seen plenty of men shanghaied in my own premises on Kearney Street, but the idea that I should be thus whisked off myself took a bit of swallowing. However, here I was, bound for God-knows-where in a ship I'd never seen! It didn't exactly suit my convenience to be thus summarily treated and I resolved there and then to do what I could to make skipper and crew regret their rash action. I was pretty certain at the same time that they had been put up to it by someone who had a grudge against me, but, of course, I never discovered who it was.

The three of us staggered a little unsteadily towards the galley (whose location was easily exposed from the smell), where we were given something that passed for food and a drink of water. The cook, a tubby little man with a round red face and an enormous hairy chest, never spoke a word as he handed me my rations. I suppose he was expecting us. The only reply I got to my impolite queries as to my whereabouts was a solemn wink. Later on we grew to be quite good pals.

After that we went on deck to look for the mate. By the look of them my fellow shanghaiees were sailormen, and I don't think the mere fact of finding themselves involuntarily back in a job worried them a great deal, but I was never cut out for a sailor and didn't intend to start then. Matters were further complicated by the fact that I found myself in a battered old hulk of a three-masted barque, square-rigged on the fore and main, and I had about as much idea of 'curling 'em up' as the mate had of busting broncos.

I told him as much when he had packed the other two off, and felt my spirits revive with the fresh air as I said it. He was a big fellow, the first, one of the old-fashioned bucko mates who never get a master's ticket, and before I left the boat we had 'words' on more than one occasion. This was the first time, for I hadn't forgiven him for that kick. A short conversation ensued first of all. It was something like this:

Mate. So here y'are, me little unprintable and its my job to turn you into a sailor.

D. McH. I'll see you in hell first. I don't know a thing about sailing except that all sailors are dirty so-and-sos.

Mate. You goddam son-of-a——, you can cut that gab out anyway! Now get up aloft with the others!

He was about to terminate these exchanges of opinion with another kick in the ribs (for which I was well prepared to pay in the same coin) when the old man appeared. "What's all this?" he inquired.

"This yellow-livered blank refuses duty, sir," explained the mate.

"Oh," said the skipper, "afraid he might get the

giddy spasms up there, eh? All right, knock his
head off! Stove his pan in! We'll soon make a
sailor of him."

"Not unless you're a better man than you look,"
I said. But by that time I had noticed the mate
was carrying a gun, stuck in his belt, and decided
to reserve my arguments for the time being.

My chance came a few hours later when they
relieved the watch. The bucko mate was evidently
determined to haze the spirit out of me, and I was
as determined to put him on the ground like a man
just as soon as I could. Before he could play any
tricks with his gun I caught him squarely in the
solar plexus and then swung him an upper to the
jaw. To my intense pleasure, he went down like a
ninepin. I guess he must have thought I was an
odd sort of sailor. But I'll give him credit. He
sure was a tough handful. So, for that matter,
were the second and the Old Man. The latter
popped his head out when he heard the rumpus.
He separated us by the simple expedient of swinging
his boot behind my ear, and nearly splitting my
skull!

I won't repeat what he said to me, and as it is
incapable of paraphrasing I must leave it to the
reader's imagination.

I never got a chance to get at the mate again. He
gave me my orders with one hand on the butt of
that gun, and I had learned sufficient of seafaring

methods to know that he would not hesitate to use it. However, after a few days of persistent 'passive resistance' and 'dumb insolence' I think I must have convinced the Old Man that I was not going to make the sailor he thought. He called me one day and told me precisely what was in his mind about land-lubberly blanks like myself. He concluded by consigning me promptly to hell and the ship's galley, which I discovered was much the same thing. It was clever, that idea. I believe the skipper and the first must have worked it out between them, because while I had been rather popular with the rest of the crew for daring to voice my grievances in no uncertain terms, I now became an object of universal hatred! When I took over from the ship's cook, he said to me: "Mac, I guess you think you're landing a soft job down here. Take it from me, matey, you'll be wishing you'd stayed on deck inside a couple of days." I thought he was kidding when he said that, because they put him to work with the rest in my place. Just cooking seemed to me a very pleasant means of whiling away the time until I could get ashore.

I had learned by now we were on the *Sacramento*, bound for Sydney with a general cargo, via the islands, but the Old Man wasn't taking any chances with that crew. No one was allowed ashore until we reached Sydney—a matter of rather over 6,000 miles out of 'Frisco. It took that sailing ship about three months, and I don't believe I was ever more wretched in my life.

I told you I thought I had struck it easy when they put me in the caboose, but it wasn't long before I found that my friend the cook wasn't kidding. I could have cooked all right if I had had any material to work upon, but the conditions on the *Sacramento* were just about as bad as anything I'd struck. The grub in the hobo jungles was twenty times better. In addition to weevils in the flour, mouldy biscuits and salt pork I wouldn't have offered a dog, the whole place was alive with cockroaches and, at night, rats.

Despite my genuine efforts it was impossible to disguise all the drawbacks simultaneously, and all through the boat from the fo'c'sle to the after-deck they cursed the cook. Not the grub, mind you, but me!

There was hardly a man aboard who didn't at some time during the voyage attempt to settle his grievance about my cooking with me personally, but without wishing to appear boastful I managed to retain my reputation as a tough guy even if I had not established it as a *cordon bleu*. (The reader will probably have concluded by now that my middle name is Fight, and I suppose that's not far from the truth. There must be something in heredity, I guess.)

We made Sydney Harbour in ninety-two days, of which I had been unconscious half the time, and my

first sight of Australia gave me an immense feeling
of relief. I knew we were going ashore there, and
wild horses wouldn't drag me back aboard the
Sacramento, especially as I thought I should have a
few dollars in my pocket.

There were three or four of us who had got
together in the evening and discussed a certain plan
I had in mind. There were two other men who had
been brought aboard in 'Frisco by the same means
as myself and a couple of other big fellows, an Irishman and a Skiwegian, who had found the skipper's
and the mate's idea of discipline a little too irksome.
They were pretty keen to wipe off a few old scores
once we set foot on dry land, and like myself were
nursing a grudge with their sore ribs.

However, before going ashore there was the
question of money to be settled. To my surprise,
the morning we dropped anchor I found that even
there I was to be disappointed. I went to the Old
Man and insisted that I should be given the money
I was entitled to at the usual rates, only to be met
with the reply that the owners always signed on
men for the *round trip!* I should be paid off when
we made 'Frisco on the return voyage. That was
a smart idea, too, if you think about it. I suppose
the skipper was pretty sure the whole darned crew
would jump the ship at Sydney after living for three
months in that hell; he and the mate would then
sign on a fresh complement, and pay them off in

San Francisco for the *single voyage*. Half the wages received from the owners would go into their pockets. I began to realise that there was method in their unnecessarily brutal treatment of the whole crew.

"But I want to go ashore," I told him.

"I'm not stopping you," he said grinning. "But you won't get a cent until we reach Golden Gates and that's owner's orders."

That settled it. I left him, but with the thought in my mind that those terms weren't good enough by a long way for me.

I saw my mates before we went ashore and we agreed to hang about until nightfall, keeping an eye on the skipper's movements, and when he made for the docks to return to the ship we would make a neat little job of paying ourselves.

We noticed they went ashore together, the Old Man and the mate, and all that afternoon we kept discreetly on their tracks. I had borrowed a pound of nails from Chips, and wrapped them in a bandana. It was an inconspicuous and serviceable weapon in case of necessity. What we were more anxious to do, though, was to relieve them of their artillery and then fight them like men, although they didn't deserve it. For three whole months I had itched to graze my knuckles on their jaws. . . .

It was about midnight when they appeared, and pretty quiet around that quarter. We had hit upon the plan of allowing two of us to go ahead and act

F

drunk. It was pretty certain that the skipper and
the mate would stop and speak to them as they
caught up. They would wonder where the men had
got the money for a skinful! The remaining two
of us would then come up behind and slug them
cold, in order to relieve them of any dangerous
weapons.

The plan worked like a charm. I saw to it I was
one of the 'operating' members, and I didn't take
any chances. The pair of them went right out for
about five minutes.

We got them on their feet, and as it had been
my idea I had the privilege of first go. I chose
the mate. He looked even nastier than before when
I had finished with him. We left the pair of them
on their backs at last, after collecting their guns and
as much of our wages as we could find. It was all
I could do to stop the Irishman from jumping on
their faces.

Rough justice, perhaps, but eminently satisfying.

II

I didn't take very kindly to Sydney as a town.
My one thought was to get back to San Francisco
and "The Thousand Delights". I wrote a letter
home explaining what had happened, but whether
it ever arrived or not, I don't know. Fate had other
plans in store for me and the next time I saw my
saloon, many years later, it was a soft drinks and

shoe-shine parlour, with a bunch of cute blonde soda-jerkers substituted for my pugilistic bar-helps!

As you may imagine, after the affair with the *Sacramento's* officers, I was anxious to get out of Sydney before the attentions of the police made a prolonged stay in the city unavoidable. Apart from which, I was not too well provided with money and it was a case of getting aboard a boat and re-crossing the Pacific as soon as possible. I hung about as long as I dared, but without success. The best I could manage was to sign on as a deck hand in an old iron tramp running from Sydney to Bombay. I decided to make the passage and chance getting a run across the Pacific on her return to Sydney.

I soon found there wasn't much to choose between my new berth and the one on the *Sacramento.* Certainly there was not so much 'discipline' of the type I had been accustomed to—as a matter of fact the skipper of the tramp was a psalm-singing Englishman by the name of Mallowes, who nevertheless made the practice of Christianity a strictly personal affair. The men's quarters were filthy, the food worse, and the heat in the tropics on her iron plates sent three of the crew off their heads.

Without going further into a lot of detail, I will merely state that conditions on that boat were sufficiently bad to make me resolve to skip once more as soon as we reached Bombay, and I hope I have convinced the reader by now that I was not a man to squeal at a little discomfort!

Two days before we reached Bombay I was taken sick with fever. I cursed my luck because I could feel, in my lucid moments, my vitality steadily ebbing. I made as little of it as I could, as I was afraid if the Quarantine Officer came aboard I should lose my chance of escape. We were due to lie off Bombay by the Oyster Rock for a week, and I was firmly determined to get ashore somehow and stay there until the boat had left again.

How I managed it I don't know to this day. It must have been a perfect example of the triumph of mind over matter! But get ashore I did and what was more amazing, I was picked up in one of the native bazaars half a mile from the water-front. My next recollection after the stifling fo'c'sle was the luxurious ease and cool interior of the house of Edeljibhoy Mukerjee, principal of the firm of that name, merchants and contractors in the city of Bombay.

CHAPTER VII

BOMBAY

I

IF I had had a spell of bad luck for the best part of a year since I left 'Frisco, the wheel had turned in my favour at last. I was soon to discover how fortunate I was to be rescued and cared for by a Parsee family. It was my first experience of any Indians other than the half-caste lascar scum which I had encountered on the water-fronts, and I was astonished to find how exceptionally generous-minded and amiable were the folks who had imposed on themselves the role of my hosts. The Parsee, I discovered, teaches benevolence as the first principle of his religion, and no man practises it more liberally. The Parsee beggar is non-existent, for such a scandalous state of affairs would not be allowed to occur in their small community. Apart from these considerations I have always found them more liberally-minded and far less bigoted than any other Asiatic, and it was due to the fact that they have no absurd restrictions on the activity of their womenfolk that the ministrations of Mukerjee's wife enabled me to make a fairly quick recovery. Mukerjee himself was a middle-aged man with, of course, a perfect knowledge of English, and as soon as I was able to give some sort of account of myself he suggested that rather than report my presence to the British authorities or the American Consul, I might care to stay with him until I could get word from San Francisco. There was, he said, a little office work to be done, if I would care to try my hand at it in return for his hospitality.

Naturally I agreed, as nothing would suit my convenience better. I had no inclination to be summarily packed off as a "distressed American citizen" especially as in the course of checking up my identity one or two unpleasant incidents might come to light.

I therefore wrote off to Inez explaining, without much hope of being believed, how I had managed to stray so far from home. I had not been with Mukerjee long when I began to realise that I didn't mind very much whether I got a reply or not. I seemed somehow on the threshold of a new life, poles apart from all my old associations in the States, and (remember I was still only 27) the prospect pleased me. I had little idea then that I was thinking quite so clearly into the future!

During my convalescence I had a chance to look round the city into which I had made such an extraordinary entry. My first and lasting impression was the dry, acrid smell which pervaded everything. Every city, of course, has its own individual smell— generally unpleasant—which to the returning wanderer is sweeter than all the perfumes of Araby. Even to-day that smell is in my nostrils, and I have come to have a sentimental affection for it. To me it is India.

I had heard, naturally, many tales of the country from sailors in the water-front saloons of 'Frisco, good travellers' tales of mysterious happenings, intrigues, magic, hypnotism and all the rest, but taken them with several large pinches of salt. I'm afraid my early upbringing had given me what might be termed a "show-me" mind, and I didn't credit much of what I heard, nor half of what I saw either! As a matter of fact, this particular principle of mine served me well on a later occasion, which if the reader will bear with me, I will relate here and now. It happened when I had been in India some considerable time and I was in the city of Peshawar, where I had made many friends, both European and Indian. I had got to know, through the white commandant, several native officers in the Khyber Militia, mostly *zemindars*, landowners, men of some substance, and, above all, gentlemen. They all have a long fighting tradition behind them up there, and in the intervals of tribal peace, many of them take a term of service with the Frontier force mentioned, policing the border for the British.

One evening I was in their lines, sitting outside with about half a dozen of their officers chatting about things of interest (I was by this time speaking the language almost as one of them, which I think helped toward my welcome) when up walked a big, burly Afridi, a little unsteady on his feet, scowling and grim-faced. He was *nushar*, a little drunk, not on alcohol (the Law of the Prophet Mahommed does not permit that), but on smoke, hasheesh, and in a bad mood. He stood scowling for a few minutes, and then growled out: "*Feringhee* (white man)—you —you and your white women—your *Belait* (England), any *bhungi* (literally 'untouchable') who has the fare money, or whose father has stolen it, can go to your country and become a gentleman, and if he has any money can buy and marry anyone of your shameless white women."

There was dead silence as I looked at him, then around at the others. There was the insult direct, intentional. What could I do? I could feel the madness rising and nearly choking me and my fingers were itching to knock him down. "Smash him," was yelling inside me but if I did, it would be simple enough in his condition, I knew. However, I was in the company of gentlemen and I knew also that these men, as the Chinese, would sooner be hacked to pieces than be held up to ridicule. If I assaulted him the insult would be paid but not forgotten; I should assert my honour as a man but just as a bazaar brawler might do it. I was anxious not to lose their respect, so I said quietly:

"Oh Man, when I looked at you I took you to be a man of this country. I did not know that you, too, were a foreigner, and that you had travelled far. I did not think you were so wise and knew so many things. How long were you in my country? How did you learn these things, O wise one?"

He answered: "I have never been to your country, may it be for ever defiled, but I know these things because I have been told."

"So," I said gently, "you have never been there, and you were told this. You, a *man!* Listen *kamakla* (fool), do you not know that in my country a child of not more than seven years would have more brains than to repeat what he had only *heard* as truth? He even knows that he can only believe half of what he sees, and you, a grown man, come among men and open your mouth thus 'You heard this, you heard that.'"

If there was silence before, it was even tenser now. Then from my friends came the murmur: "*Shabash ah shabashee* (Bravo, oh bravo)."

Perhaps it was just as well the fellow didn't have his knife or gun with him. You have to see the look of hate on the face of an Afridi to appreciate it! His was good as he walked away. We resumed our interrupted talk, no mention being made of what had just happened.

But to resume: I had certainly never imagined myself in my wildest dreams actually in India, least of all witnessing the 'wonders', but here I was, and although I did not know it, for a good slice of my life. It's difficult to generalise about a country of four hundred million people, but a superficial impression is best summed up in the words of a friend I made there. He describes it not as the mysterious East, but the home of every horror that crawls and flies, the land of heat, brass chatties and stinks! And, up to a point, he was right.

At first I found everything around me so strange that I used to stand and rock with laughter. I shall never forget my first glimpse of a Bombay policeman, standing solemn as an owl, full of importance under his umbrella, with a yellow and blue hat like a pancake and chin-strap, blue smock and knee-length pants, skinny legs and feet on a wooden block which he held by a knot which came up between his first two toes!

After years of associating law and order with the blue-uniformed United States 'cop', I just had to howl with laughter. One characteristic, however, all policemen seem to share, and all the music-hall jokes in the world have never altered it, and that is the size of their feet! Even in the short trousers and wooden sandals they were unmistakably 'coppers' dogs'.

I was chiefly interested in the native bazaars,

of course, and spent many hours watching the butchers squatting on their heels cut their meat by holding the knife between their toes and sawing the meat on the blade, and seeing the cobblers winding the waxed thread round their big toe. I was amazed also to see the native wood-turners, men, incidentally, of extraordinary skill, using right hand and bow string for turning power, left hand for the tool, and, as I live, their great toe as a chuck. I mention these aspects of bazaar-life particularly, as I am one of those unfortunates who are particularly sensitive about the feet. A cold chill would chase down my spine as I watched these strange manipulations of the native toe.

I visited the native theatre once or twice but the naïve fairy stories with 'actors' being swung about on very obvious wires without any attempt at concealment were too much for my western sophistication. When I had mastered Hindustani, months later, I was a little more amused.

It never struck me as strange at the time that I should be working for a native. My idea of a coloured man was either a United States negro, or a greaser, and the Parsees filled neither role. The Mukerjees lived in a European-style bungalow out on the Malabar Hill not far from the Elephanta Caves, and as he was a man of some substance there was, of course, none of the squalor and poverty which I associated with 'niggers'; in fact, I had never lived in such a well appointed house in my life. About three weeks after my arrival I went down to the offices of Edeljibhoy Mukerjee and Sons on the Bund Road at the edge of the Bazaar, and was initiated into the mysteries of book-keeping. The three sons worked in the business with the old man, but as they were often in different parts of the country buying for the firm I did not see a great deal of them. When we did meet, however, they were always extremely cordial and friendly.

My first day in the office I was a little startled to see the native clerk sitting *on* the counter, cross-legged, with a desk in front of him. The cashier there was a remarkable man, too. He had reduced simple addition to such a fine art that he was able to tell by weighing in his hand the exact amount of rupee silver he was counting, and in some mysterious manner could instantly detect the not infrequent presence of counterfeit pieces.

It soon became evident to me if I was to be of any real use in the business that I should have to learn Hindustani. I mentioned my intention to Mukerjee who seemed very pleased to think that I should take my obligations so seriously. As time went on and I did not hear from America, I became steadily less inclined to bother about my return and the prospect of settling in India became an accepted fact. For the first time in my life I was in a settled job—I elicited that from my employer—and although in strange circumstances I was comfortable and happy. Once my system had become acclimatised to the intense heat, I felt perfectly fit and, above all, interested.

The old man gave me every opportunity of learning the language, even to allowing me one whole day a week to wander about the bazaars airing my tongue with natives, which, of course, is the best way of learning any language. I was surprised at my own progress, discovering quite accidentally that I had a natural aptitude for languages which subsequently was more than once the means of saving my life.

At the same time I was learning to control myself, largely for the sake of my employer, and during the whole of my stay in Bombay I was only in trouble once. On that occasion I beat a *gharrywallah* for what I considered insolence, and was reported to the magistrate and fined. I was thankful that so little fuss was made, because I was still rather apprehensive of the consequence of any sort of 'investigation' into my identity. However, Mukerjee did not seem to think much the worse of me for my indiscretion, informing me that the year before a European had killed a native outright in Green's Café in Bombay and was eventually fined five rupees for his misdemeanour! At the same time I took good care to avoid any further unpleasantness, especially as I had been promised, as soon as I became really proficient in Hindustani, that I should be sent on buying expeditions for the firm in various parts of the country. I should explain that we were general merchants dealing in almost every commodity from carpets to corn, and bales of silk to consignments of camels. Mukerjee did quite a lot of business with the Government and I fancy that he considered it very much in the interests of the firm to have an American on his buying staff.

Living with them as I did, I grew to have a genuine affection for the whole family and a healthy respect for their religious observances. The 'heathen' aspect of the followers of Zoroaster was soon lost in admiration for their code of life and even the actual ceremonial of the faith. In particular I was impressed by their methods of burial, after I had been privileged to attend a relative's funeral with my employer.

A Parsee is always born on the ground floor of a house, since only by good word and deed can he attain a more elevated position in either world! And it is on the ground floor that the last rites begin. I believe only male friends and relatives attend the funeral. After the body had been dressed in a clean robe of the whitest linen, it was placed upon the bier and covered from head to foot. (No coffin is used, since burial in the Western sense is not permitted.) Then the attendant priests formed a procession of mourners, headed by themselves, and the body was carried to the *Dakhma* or Tower of Silence on the Malabar Hill. A number of these 'towers' are situated in a lovely park on the summit of the hill surrounded by tall trees. It is in those trees that there live multitudes of what to Western eyes may have a rather sinister significance—vultures! But the Parsee regards them in a different light entirely. They have a grisly function to perform on such occasions and are considered part and parcel of the ceremony. The *Dakhma* itself is a stone tower about 30 feet high with a small door at the foot. In this the bier was placed, and there left until the flesh was picked from the bones by the flocks of birds. This last resting-place is so constructed that the bones fall through a grid in a pit beneath whence they are taken and cremated in the *Bahram-atish* or Temple of Fire where the sacred fires burn eternally. After prayers it is usual to hand the priest a list of charities to which the mourners have subscribed in memory of their dead. So once again I was to see how the idea of philanthropy occupies the Parsee from birth to death. The longer I lived among them the more I felt that so-called Christians might well take a leaf out of their book.

II

It was after I had been in Bombay about six months that I conceived a notion which, crazy though it was, altered the whole course of my life. It arose originally out of my desire to perfect my Hindustani.

Instead of being merely conversant, I wanted to be certain that I spoke literally like a native. There was one certain method of assuring myself about this and that was to discard European dress and go into the native quarter as one of them. I expect this idea will horrify any *pukka sahib* who chances to read it, but without attempting to excuse myself, let me state that I was neither English nor public-school, and had no notions about the prestige of the white man to deter me.

I realised, of course, that detection would probably land me into trouble, but trouble was something to which I had become fairly accustomed. Accordingly, and with the approval of old Mukerjee, I began to go regularly at nights, clad in a *dhoti*, into the parts of the city where Europeans are not particularly welcome. For a time I had to keep my mouth well closed, but my boldness increased with my proficiency in Hindustani and to my great joy I found that I could pass undetected as a genuine native. My skin at this time was only tanned and for that reason I never ventured to go out dressed like that in the daytime. At night, however, it was fairly simple, and I made a regular practice of it. Naturally, I first took some pains to acquire native mannerisms and peculiarities of dress, and spent hours learning idiom, distinguishing the various castes and classes, watching carefully the way in which a man wound his puggaree round his head.

I dressed myself like any poorly-clad Mahommedan, insignificant and unnoticed.

To anyone who has never threaded the crowded native bazaars after nightfall—and there are few white men who dare—it is an unforgettable experience. The first two or three times I was revolted by the stifling, dirty, nauseating heat. The appalling squalor and the collection of unsavoury smells appals the western senses in a manner impossible to describe. Even when I had learned to identify individual smells, garlic, *ghee*, spices, incense and rotten meat and a hundred others, the combination of them all defies description other than the world's worst stench!

However, I was not going to allow myself to be deterred by superficial discomforts and in the dim, hot obscurity I used to wander round, drinking a cup of coffee here, buying sweetmeats there, conversing with the shopkeepers by the charcoal fires. The stench of the rag floating in a saucer of cocoanut oil, which usually served as the only form of illumination would make me retch sometimes, but I stuck it, realising the unpleasant consequences of discovery. Many of the shopkeepers would lie asleep in the street outside their 'premises' on a quilted rug, a blanket over their heads to keep away evil spirits, or snore on a charpoy just inside, in full view of passers-by. The noise of chatter, singing, and music would go on without ceasing through

G

the night. Someone would be playing a zitka to the ceaseless throb of a palm-beaten drum, while in shrill discord a singer would sustain a note for so long that it seemed impossible that his lungs would not burst. It struck me as strange, this capacity for drawn-out notes in spite of the fact that nearly all natives smoke from childhood. The communal pipe, hookah or red clay, was a regular feature of an evening's entertainment in which I often joined when I felt I could safely sit down and talk and eat and take my turn at a smoke. When I first heard the "*Hene puckarao*,[1] brother; pull deep for smoke is good when a man is full and resting," I knew I was accepted.

My object in these 'native' excursions was really to get behind the native mind, as well as master his tongue, and while I do not claim to have succeeded entirely, at least this gave me plenty of opportunity for investigation. I was anxious, too, not to feel that the native was 'taking a rise out of me'—which he delights in doing to any sahib, since if I was to hold my job I knew I had to strike a proper bargain for my employer.

One morning Mukerjee called me into one side of his office to introduce me to one of his business associates. I found myself confronted by a tall, elderly man, of very aristocratic bearing, whose loose white *camees*, wide trousers and long-pointed,

[1] Take it.

shoes of red and green leather revealed him as a
Pathan from the northern provinces. I noticed, too,
that he was a hajji, his green puggaree with its high
red conical centre cap shewing he had made the
pilgrimage to Mecca. His name was Sherif Ali, a
merchant from the frontier city of Peshwar, and
when I first saw him I little realised how well we
were to come to know each other.

"This is the man, hajji," Mukerjee told him,
pointing to me, "I am thinking of sending up to
you. He is even as my own son. Do you think he
is fit for the work?"

The fierce old bearded face turned to me, the
eyes ranging me up and down as he answered:
"He seems to be good, in God's name. Speak, my
son. You have the language of this part of the
country well enough, I hear. But what tongue is
that? is it loose, like a woman's, or does it not wag
until the moment is ripe? We in the north have a
saying "A loose tongue is a cut throat in the dawn."
You are wanted for work that is both good and
profitable, but have you learned the speech of the
Pushtu?"

I tried to answer him matching his own words
and arrogant manner, tempered with the respect
due to his age. "Mine is a man's tongue, hajji;
I leave talk to women. As for Pushtu, at present
I cannot speak it but *bat*[1] comes easily enough to me.

[1] Languages.

Is the tongue of the North so terrible that you think to frighten me by merely mentioning it? I fear no man, far less a language!"

Mukerjee turned to him: "A few months should suffice, my good friend," he said. "As you hear he speaks well enough. It will be as well to teach him, and he is an apt pupil."

"What am I supposed to do up there, *mera bap?*" I asked Mukerjee, wondering what it was all about.

He smiled rather mysteriously and then said casually: "Just the usual purchases, *mera butcha.* Grain, chiefly. But you understand the majority of the population up there speaks only Pushtu. They seem to despise the poor Hindu. A different people."

I knew this to be true, of course, having been in India long enough to learn why the British stationed a large force in the north-west.

"It is well," said Sherif Ali. "We shall perhaps meet again, then." With that I went out and left them.

I think I can say without lack of modesty that I had made myself fairly useful by this time to the firm for which I was working and was frequently sent out of Bombay up and down the country in the role of buyer. This, of course, entailed a considerable amount of travelling, which I did not neglect to put to good use in further making myself familiar with the ways and habits of the Indian native. Train travel in India is like no other that I have experienced in the world. The first few occasions I journeyed back and forth as a sahib, that is to say in the comparative comfort of a shaded, airy compartment, with all the convenience of being converted into a pullman for night travel. However, although I met with a fair amount of business success, I soon became aware that in all India there are two prices for any commodity—one for the sahib, the other for the native. I therefore suggested to Mukerjee that if he agreed I was quite prepared to travel as a native in a little less luxury, since I felt it would be in the interests of the firm. He laughed at the idea and told me to try it once if I liked. He didn't think there would be a second time!

I shan't forget that first adventurous trip in a hurry. I thought I might as well start from the bottom and I went as a poor native at that, travelling in a carriage (save the word!) reserved for Indians. I've heard of *Dante's Inferno*, of course, but if it beats that one, I'll take the trouble to read it! All the same, the reader must believe me when I say that after that first time I always travelled like that, and what's more I enjoyed it. I must point out again that at this stage I was now heat-proof, stench-proof (almost) and mosquito-proof. These beasts simply won't bite me for a reason I've never discovered, but the fact remains and that is why, I suppose, I never got malaria. I was not, however, quite louse-proof and I must confess that at first this feature of native travel proved a little irksome. Short of being destroyed, I don't think these native compartments on the Indian Railways could ever be entirely freed from this menace, since generations of travellers have brought them in on their persons, and a popular means of wasting time during the journey is getting rid of them. Not, mind you, killing them, for the native has no grudge against lice, considering them one of God's creatures with the rest and part of the eternal Scheme of Things. In this frame of mind they are merely removed from the person and sent to seek another home! However, once accustomed to this rather objectionable feature, there are many compensations for the mode of travel I chose. Sometimes there would be a compartment packed with men, women and squalling brats in an atmosphere which baffles description, chattering, laughing (and not infrequently spitting), smoking hubble-bubbles and eating; and there was one occasion on which I heard for the first time two native women quarrelling, one at each end of a long compartment. They were experts, these two, although what it was about I never determined. They had probably forgotten, too, in the heat and enjoyment of abusing each other. They made no attempt at physical contact but just sat there howling at each other from opposite ends, at first above the general babble of talk, but eventually by sheer lung power forcing their fellow-travellers, including myself, into comparatively silent but highly amused spectators. Sailors and Billingsgate fishwives would wonder why they ever thought they could handle language if they heard Indian women. As we heard each thrust and parry of the wordy duel, the rest of the occupants yelled wild applause. How long it would have gone on I don't know, but it was fully an hour before the train stopped and we all piled out. I enjoyed every minute of it, and when we stopped I would get on the platform with the rest and, having no caste principles, buy any and everything from the foodwallahs who sold their wares to the hungry travellers. I could eat food cooked by anyone— good hot cakes, bowls of mutton curry, curds and sweets. Occasionally I would treat myself to the luxury of a cigarette but for the most part I preferred to stand my share of tobacco for the compartment pipe, which I carried tied in a corner of my rags with the few annas I brought to pay for it all.

Of course I travelled with a case full of clean kit further up the train with the rest of my luggage in charge of my boy, a middle-aged Pathan whom I had selected not only for his qualities as a good servant but partly because he was dumb, having lost his tongue in one of the pleasant little blood-feuds his people were so fond of. In any case I don't think there was much fear of his 'talking' as I had put the fear of Allah into him when he saw me at work with my hands once in a bazaar brawl. One of his own countrymen had come at me with a knife and I had broken his arm to get it, subsequently using it on its owner, I'm afraid.

And so it went on, for I suppose about six months after my interview with Mukerjee and his friend, during which time not another word was spoken about the possibility of my going North. Indeed I had almost forgotten about it when one day Mukerjee said:

"I think you had better go up to Peshawar City next week, my son. Do you want to?"

There was nothing I wanted more. That brief interview with Sherif Ali had aroused my anticipations, although perhaps I have not conveyed it very well. I received a definite impression that there was something in the wind besides general merchanting. In the meanwhile, however, I had made a few inquiries about the frontier city and elicited some interesting facts.

"Of course I want to go, my father," I said, "but isn't it true that civilian Europeans are not encouraged to enter the city itself?"

"As a matter of fact, they're strongly discouraged by the authorities," replied the old man, "and that is precisely why I want you to go there. You will, of course, be engaged in buying merchandise for me in Peshawar Cantonment—I will give you your instructions later about that—but at the same time you will be acting in the capacity of private enquiry agent."

This sounded more interesting and I pressed for details.

"I would rather not tell you too much until you are actually in the city," he said. "It's a sore subject with the British authorities, but at the same time it is a business which has considerable financial possibilities. At all events I wish you to get as much detail as you can, as I have been asked to finance a deal and I will only undertake it if I have your assurance that there are some prospects of success."

"But what *is* it?" I asked again.

"This much I can tell you," said Mukerjee, "although you probably know it already, and you must draw your own conclusions. His Highness the Amir of Afghanistan is reputed to be employing several European engineers in his arsenal at Kabul. At the same time, numbers of his less orderly subjects are permanently engaged in border raids—not for gold or to take human life—although I believe that is often incidental—but to procure the service-rifles provided by the King-Emperor to his brave troops stationed on the border. In fact, beyond the north-west frontier, firearms stand at a premium." He smiled at me, and I could see it was useless at that moment to carry the conversation further. Most things in the East are spoken of by inference.

I had heard enough in any case to make mere

interest change to excitement. "I have heard something of the sort, my father," I said, and there let
the matter drop.

As a matter of fact, the 'something of the sort'
that I had heard was a collection of most interesting
stories from various sources about life on the border.
While I was in Bombay I struck up a casual acquain-
tance with a fellow named Haynes, an I.C.S. engineer
who had been working up there for several years,
and when we met sometimes for a drink at the Taj
Mahal Hotel he would often intrigue me for days
after with his descriptions of the type of man he had
to deal with up there.

"They're as different," he told me once, "from
the down-country Hindu as chalk from cheese, these
border tribesmen. In fact the ordinary servile,
coolie-minded Hindu doesn't care about going north
of Pindi. The first time I went up there my khitmitgar
suddenly remembered on Pindi station his father
was dying and left me there and then. I was dealing
with Afridis largely and a more arrogant, prouder
lot of fighting devils you'll never meet. They don't
value human life above a tinker's cuss. They're
all born with the idea that the next man's only waiting
for a chance to knock 'em off, and they act accordingly.
The very way they walk seems to reflect their insolent
manner. There's no sort of respect for the white
man except in his ability as a fighting unit. Most
of their lives are spent in avenging blood feuds.

For anything resembling an insult the Afridi will willingly spend his life in wiping out every man-jack of the family who gave it. They're always armed, across the frontier. Rifles generally, and of course knives—they used a wicked looking thing called a *peshkoza* up there and artists at it, too. They worry more about ammunition for their guns than food for their bellies. Of course, they have to make their own or get someone else's. I remember one fellow up in the Khyber country telling me quite as a matter of fact that he was a bit short of rupee silver once and lay up with the idea of picking off the next man he saw. He was down to his last round of *goli-baroot*[1] and that means he was hard up. Well, without going into details, he got his man, and when he came down and rolled him over, the poor devil had three pice on him and it costs four annas to make a cartridge! Was that Afridi mad? He didn't care a hoot about killing the man. All that he was worried about was wasting his last cartridge."

On another occasion he said: "Afghanistan's a queer country. Did you ever hear about Harrison? He took a chance and got away with it. There's plenty of opportunity up there for a white man who can get through and doesn't value his life too highly."

"Who was Harrison?" I asked him.

"A second-rate musician," he said. "He was in Kabul for five years and came away with a packet of

[1] Ammunition.

money. It seems that the Amir had sent a message through to the commandant at Peshawar asking if they would recommend a band-master as he was reforming his army and felt that martial music was a thing to have. The word was duly spread that there was a safe conduct to Kabul through the Khyber for anyone who felt like taking the job. If the Amir wasn't satisfied, of course, the British authorities didn't vouch for the consequences. Well, a little man named Harrison volunteered. I'm not sure what he was doing up there. He had an interest in some silk firm, I think. Anyway he went up through the Khyber, complete with wife, and nobody heard anything of him for five years. It was a pretty good certainty he'd had his throat cut, as the Amir had the reputation of not wasting time in shewing his displeasure. But anyway he arrived back in Peshawar five years later worth about half a million rupees, and his wife so weighed down with jewels she couldn't walk! Oh yes, there's a chance to make boodle in Kabul, if you can only get there."

"But surely the Amir doesn't want band-masters all the time?" I asked.

Haynes laughed. "No," he said. "But it's always the army he's thinking about. White officers for troop-training, white engineers for the gun-factory. But naturally the British authorities want to keep Afghanistan as short of anything like that as possible. They're enough trouble as it is.

If they ever got properly organised, God help India!"

It was stories like these that I remembered when Mukerjee told me I was going north on business. Things were looking up, I felt.

Only one further reference was made to the object of my departure before I left. Mukerjee said to me one morning: "It is as well, my son, that you are soon leaving the city of Bombay."

"Why so?" I asked him.

"Word has reached me," he told me, "that your presence here has not remained entirely unnoticed by the authorities and I'm afraid that some sort of investigation, although purely formal, may be made shortly. From what you once told me, although a matter of indifference to me, I feel it would be as well if you went elsewhere, and moreover assumed a different identity." He smiled as he told me this and added: "I have had some cards printed for you for business purposes. You will find that for present purposes you are to be Mr. Roberts, my agent in the Punjaub and the Northern Provinces."

I couldn't help laughing to myself when I left him. I was on the run again!

CHAPTER VIII

THROUGH THE KHYBER

I

THE next week I left Bombay and took a train to the North. The long hot days and nights as we crossed the plains were dull enough but as we approached Rawalpindi, my anticipations rose. In spite of Mukerjee's final reminder that I was likely to come under official surveillance again, I must confess that the prospect of a little excitement again was more than welcome, and lately in Bombay my 'itching feet' had begun to worry me. Here at last I was on the move, with new prospects, new surroundings. The fertile country of the Punjaub was refreshingly unfamiliar, and already I noticed a different type of man working in the fields. Big men, straight as laths, Sikh and Jat, ploughing with their primitive single share behind a camel and a donkey yoked together. Past Rawalpindi I began to notice a change in the atmosphere, too. It was the sharp, cool, rarified mountain air which I associated with those far off days in America, which I had almost forgotten. The train went through Attock—the old gateway of India in the days of the Russian Bear menace. By the look of things, I should think that even the Russians would have had a job to get past that gate. A bridge spans the point where the Kabul and Indus rivers meet, each buttress hollowed out and fortified, overhanging a raging Niagara of a torrent over a mile wide! As I reached Nowshera I got my first glimpse of the distant misty hills beyond which, I knew, lay the homes of the men who lived by looting and harrying—Wazirs, Orakzai, Afridi and Pathan, of whose cunning and ferocity I had heard many tales in the bazaars of Bombay.

The next stop was Pabbi, and it was there that occurred the incident which I have related elsewhere of the officer who lost his tent and belongings. They were quartered there on the way up to one of the fortified hill-stations which lie beyond.

Then, at last, Peshawar. My arrival there was something of a disappointment. The bustling crowd of Indians, servants, soldiers, porters and passengers seemed very much the same as at any other station. I had expected something different here, at the edge of the frontier, although just what I found it hard to imagine. The loose clothing of the Pathan tribesmen was substituted for the *dhoti* of the down-country Hindu, and that was all the difference I could see.

This was my first glimpse of Peshawar. My last, years later, presented a very different picture. The whole place had been recently fortified and was piled with sandbags. A few weeks before a party of raiders had come down from the hills and laid in wait for the mail train. It came in as usual, unsuspecting, and drew up in the station. Suddenly hell broke loose! The first man to go down was the guard, as he stepped out. Next, the driver, and the white fireman was nicked by a bullet as he ducked. Then came the wild sortie of tribesmen, howling and firing. But unfortunately (or the reverse) their intelligence service had let them down for once, as the mail train had been shunted down the line to allow the passage of a strong detachment of British troops, complete with ball ammunition, who tumbled out and got busy. There must have been many wailing widows in the hills that night! Not that the men themselves worried particularly about being killed. It was the best end a man could meet, and are not companies of *houris* waiting in Paradise for all true believers?

Outside the station, I got a gharry and ordered the wallah to drive to the Dak bungalow. I noticed immediately the difference between this fellow and the knockneed rats who ply for hire in Bombay. He was a Pathan. As I drove through the dusty roads lined with trees, with their orderly collection of low-built, flat-roofed bungalows each with its patch of well-kept lawn in front I caught a different view of the distant, blue-hazed hills through which I knew ran the dreaded Khyber Pass, which later was to become more familiar to me than the streets of Humboldt, California.

We drove along the 'straight' road, skirting the city up past the old fort on the North Circular Road, a continuation of the Grand Trunk which winds its 3,000 miles of highway from Calcutta to Peshawar. I explored this road later to its very end at Buraj-Hari-Singh, the site of the last Sikh-Mahommedan battle, the territorial limit of British India. Beyond that lies the five-mile stretch of open country, the No Man's Land before reaching Afghanistan proper, and which is called Yagastan. We went past the Badami Bagh in the Mall and finally reached the Dak bungalow where I found to my surprise I was expected! Somebody evidently knew I was coming and was preparing the way, for the old *chokidar* in charge informed me that I could move into my own bungalow the following day. It was now being got ready for me! Naturally I pretended this was quite in order, and the following day I moved into a large bungalow, of the usual type complete in every detail even down to the 'boy'. My old one had left me at Pindi. When he realised where we were bound he made me understand that nothing on earth would bring him to Peshawar. It was too near his own border country where the poor devil had lost his tongue! The new one turned out to be a model cook, valet and butler, beside which he was habitually as silent as the grave. My comings and goings, strange as

H

some of them were, passed apparently quite unnoticed. I hardly ever saw him in the bungalow, and yet when I wanted him he was always there, slipping his shoes off his feet outside. Never by a word or a sign did he betray surprise at my subsequent odd appearance.

Once settled in I began to look round in order to find out how I should best execute my business. This was nominally the purchase of general commodities—grain, carpets, *lungis*, woven cloth and so on in the district and also from the caravans which came down from Afghanistan regularly with all sorts of merchandise. These purchases had to be sent through to Mukerjee's go-down at Bombay and consignments made at regular intervals until I was given instructions to return. For this purpose I was well-equipped for any inquiries that might arise as to my bona-fides. My card stated:

MR. ANDREW ROBERTS
Agent
Edeljibhoy Mukerjee & Co.,
Bombay.
General Merchants

The other business to occupy my attention (and of which hardly a word had been said) was to find Sherif Ali, the carpet merchant, in the native city of Peshawar and gather any information I could. I knew this would be difficult, due to the extraordinary reticence on such subjects all over India and specially in the north, where a still tongue not only makes a wise head but is often the only thing which will keep that head on its body! I did not, however, anticipate quite such difficulty as confronted me when, a few days after my arrival, I drove the two miles from the cantonment to the walled city to find a policeman and a notice posted on every gate. The notice read:

> THE ENTRY OF EUROPEANS INTO THIS CITY IS STRICTLY FORBIDDEN. THE GOVERNMENT DOES NOT UNDERTAKE RESPONSIBILITY FOR THE LIVES OF ANY WHITE PERSONS CONTRAVENING THIS REGULATION.

So it was like that! I had rather imagined that, armed with my firm's credentials, I could get a special pass from the District Commissioner to carry out my business. It was not very encouraging and I had to devise some other plan a little less direct in order to establish contact with Sherif Ali.

I decided to wait around a while until I got the lie of the land, to see if there were any hints to be dropped by the people who lived up there permanently. The language difficulty arose again here, for apart from the Hindu shopkeepers most of the native population is Pathan and my knowledge of Pushtu at that date was very elementary.

I spent all my leisure moments exploring the cantonment and especially the Suddar Bazaar—the main, and indeed the only shopping centre of Peshawar cantonment. It was always thronged with a picturesque conglomeration of native races, Hindu merchants, grave-looking Moslems, Sikhs, Pathans, Kashmiri, savage-visaged Afridi, and a few women here and there veiled from head to foot in their white *burkhas* with their tiny eyeholes looking more like the Ku Klux Klan than anything else. And mingling with them all a fair percentage of khaki-clad soldiers from the barracks and civilian Europeans—civil servants and their wives for the most part. One aspect of the bazaar used to afford me a certain improper delight. Any European who goes on his first shopping expedition in the cantonment naturally orders the gharry-wallah to drive to the Suddar Bazaar, and as naturally (with a sense of impish mischief which never failed to amuse me, I'm afraid!) is duly dropped at the far end. This is the notorious Red Lamp quarter, and the shrill screams of the brazen courtesans yelling innumerable impolite suggestions were, of course, a source of terrible embarrassment to anyone who happened to bring his wife.

It was during these expeditions to the bazaar that I began to realise what I had already found to be true of India further south was even truer here. It is difficult to describe the difference of approach to life generally of the native compared to the westerner. Every aspect of everyday existence is inextricably bound up in a sort of mysterious secrecy, an underhand indirectness of speech and behaviour.

A spade is never called a spade under any circumstances—in fact is never referred to except by the most circuitous method of speech which only those who are constantly in contact with the native mind can ever unravel. The right hand never knows what the left is doing. Always there seems some underlying fear, a deep-down mistrust of fellowmen, born possibly of centuries of oppression, which forced me to the conclusion that all India lives in peril of its life. The 'mysterious East' is not such a misnomer after all. The whole of India seems one vast underworld. Men disappear for no reason. A word too much is spoken and perhaps it is the last.

I have gone to some length to explain this as maybe it will help the reader to understand some of my difficulty in ever getting beneath the surface, and when I did do so, of the impossibility of explaining how. A veiled hint here, a vague suggestion there was all I had to go on. The fact that the native city of Peshawar was forbidden territory only made me more determined to get in, and a few weeks after my first disappointment I tried again. I was naturally more than a little apprehensive after the awful warnings and the tales that I had since heard of what went on inside the walls, but I was determined to reach Mukerjee's friend, Sherif Ali, the merchant of carpets.

My chance came unexpectedly. I was outside the "Gate of the Camels" one morning about noon on a

tour of inspection of possible means of entry when a
company of Afghan *povindahs*[1] was passing in. There
were about thirty of them and the usual accompani-
ment of camels and donkeys. I watched them for a
minute or two before I realised that *the native policeman was no longer on the gate!* He had taken an
opportunity to leave his post, and I seized the chance
to walk through into the city bold as brass. After
what I had heard I quite expected to have my throat
cut within five minutes, although I had taken certain
steps to protect myself. On my hip was a ·45
automatic.

At last I was inside the forbidden city! The
first obstacle was surmounted and I knew now that if
I could remain unmolested until I found the house of
Sherif Ali, I should be safe as well as sound. At
sundown the city gates were closed and there would
be no getting out. Once inside, I hurried along in the
seething mass of people down the crooked streets of
flat-roofed mud houses (many with shops on the
ground floor, typical of any native bazaar). The
'shops' were small booths for the most part with an
odd collection of roofings composed of thatch,
corrugated sheet-iron and enamelled advertisements
of "Lipton's Tea" and "Singer Sewing Machines".
(I often wonder if the firms in question realise what
a wealth of free advertisement they get up and down
the length of India!) My idea was to avoid speech

[1] Travelling merchants.

until I should see some Hindu shopkeeper who might direct me or act as interpreter. I had no idea where Sherif Ali lived, but provided you know the occupation of the man you are seeking it would not be difficult in a city the size of Peshawar to find anyone, eventually. Most of the passers-by seemed to be Mahommedan Pathans, many of them tall, aquiline-featured men from across the border. For an hour I searched the city vainly, but beyond receiving a few black looks no one attempted to stop me, until at last my eye caught a bale of rugs in a little booth with the name displayed *Jasaji Singh.*

A little old man was squatting inside clad in the *dhoti* of the down-country Hindu.

"Salaam ali Koum!" I greeted him.

"Wali Kouma salaam, sahib," he returned. "We are not often honoured with the sahib's presence in this city, and I think thou art a stranger for I know not thy face." There was a meaning undertone in his voice, which, however I chose to disregard.

"I seek the house of Sherif Ali," I told him, "a wealthy merchant of rugs and carpets, although doubtless he has nothing so precious as these that lie here."

"Aye, sahib, I know him well. An honourable man and greatly respected here in Peshawar. He has many fine rugs and carpets of Kabul and Kurdistan. His shop is at the end of this street. Anyone will show you."

I thanked him and wended my way once more in the direction he indicated.

I noticed as I walked that the height of the buildings in the narrow streets was very irregular, some being as high as four stories, and many of them evidently inter-communicating. I subsequently found this peculiarity very useful in an emergency flight, since a man may enter a house at one end of a street and his pursuer will never be certain at just what point he will emerge again.

I found the shop of Sherif Ali quite easily and was not surprised to find that the largest establishment was that of the man I had met in Mukerjee's office. It was open-fronted as they all were. I did not have to enquire for him for he was sitting on a fine silk Persian rug in the centre.

He showed no sign of surprise when he saw me.

"I have come, hadji," I said.

He got up immediately and just stretched out his hands.

"Come in, sahib. Welcome to my house. Come upstairs. First thou wilt eat? After the washing, then we may talk without ears listening."

If anyone had seen him greet me thus, native and sahib, perhaps they might have thought it unusual, perhaps not thought anything about it. The *feringhee* was mad anyway, or he would not have been in there!

II

The hospitality I received at the hands of Sherif Ali was second only to that of the Mukerjees and he assured me whenever I saw him that his house was my own. I stayed with him for weeks at a time, only going back to the cantonment occasionally so as to establish my residence there and avoid any suspicion about my business.

Sherif Ali secured a tutor to make me proficient in Pushtu which I found as easy to acquire as Hindustani. It was impressed on me, however, that my identity as a *sahib* must be strictly concealed even from my teacher, with the result that I had to learn a language receiving instruction in a tongue I had not spoken eighteen months before. However, I had mastered the art of actually thinking in Hindustani, and there was little fear of detection in my accent. Besides the language, of course, there were other things I was anxious to learn—the tricks and mannerisms by which those who have the Pushtu tongue are instantly recognisable. My tutor was an old Afridi, a *spingheeri*, long-bearded and venerable, and when I explained that I wished also to learn something of Afridi manners and customs I aroused a deep suspicion which I had some difficulty in erasing. I told him that I intended to become a Mussulman, and that easily convinced him that I was worthy of his tuition. And what is more, a Mussulman I

later became and have remained to this day, for which
I shall be for ever thankful.

And so it came about that I learned the 'sittings
and the uprisings' and all manner of habits which
come as native to the Afridi, as well as the Pushtu
tongue. He told me of the eight various clans,
or *Khels*, and the way each lived, the Khuki,
the Malikdin, the Zakka, and the others. Of how the
Afridi lies shut in his tower during the day for the
whole of the year, venturing out only at night like
a beast of prey, save for the four months when the
mullah proclaims the *Kane lagawal* (the putting down
of the stone) until the *Kane utalawal* (the raising
of the stone). That is the time when a truce to all
blood-feuds and raiding is declared, and soil must be
tilled to raise the meagre crops for the year's food.
He told me of the respect for elders which is the
law of The Prophet. No man may sit until the old
ones are first seated. And many times he would tell
me of the raids of the men of his clan.

I proved an apt pupil, I think, especially as I
was impatient to get out into the city and listen to
conversation in the bazaars. At last the time came
when I considered myself sufficiently fluent to try
the Government examination in Pushtu which is held
in the cantonment and open to white civilians and
military. The reward for passing the required
standard (which is exceptionally high) is Rs. 800,
and to earn that you must certainly know Pushtu.

For the oral examination a batch of Pathans, Afghans, Afridis and other Pushtu-speaking natives is rounded up in the bazaar and you are invited to engage anyone of them in conversation. They always enter into the spirit of the thing and do their best to baffle the unfortunate examinees with slang and obscure phrases. The old Afridi I selected, I remember, I discovered to my horror as he spoke to be almost toothless, an unforeseen complication which required a certain skill and ear to overcome. Eventually I hit on a method of quelling his toothless mumblings. I insulted him. That is the one thing in this world which no Afridi will countenance.

"To what clan dost thou belong?" I asked him.

"I am of the Aka Khel," he mumbled indistinctly, and I could see from his grin he was enjoying himself. My next few questions made him change his expression, however.

"Are they not brave fighting men, skilled in the use of arms?"

"None braver, in the sight of Allah, as all men know."

"How then dost thou then belong to them? Surely thou art no warrior? Do they leave thee with the women when they go to their fighting? Dost thou protect thy feeble body behind women's skirts?"

That did it! Quite suddenly he began to enunciate extremely clearly, and even if he spoke quickly told me in no uncertain terms just what he thought of me. In a few moments the whole room was laughing and when we finished our argument I was pretty certain I had passed.

I tried this dodge of thinly veiled insult on another occasion when I was trying to get an old Afridi to talk. I had addressed one of the old men in the Suddar Bazaar on some pretext in the faint hope of eliciting some sort of information about my 'business' and the activities of the gun-merchants. He was seated on a string charpoy, apparently thinking about nothing when I greeted him in the usual manner.

"Starra ma shai!" (lit. Mayst thou not become tired), I said.

"Khwar ma shai (and thou, too), sahib."

"To what tribe dost thou belong?" I asked him.

"I am of the Khuki."

"So? And when thy clan was fighting the British wert thou, too, not fighting?"

He looked up at me for the first time. "Loose mouths belong to women and fools," he said contemptuously. "Talk without object is of no value."

I repeated my question and at length he said: "No."

"Were you then down here, away from your people?"

"No."

"Were you at home in the village?"

"No."

"And yet not fighting?"

"No."

These monosyllabic grunts were all I could get but I was determined to make him talk.

"You were with the women, perhaps?"

No answer.

"You were sick with syphilis and could not fight? Your manhood had left you?"

Then he spoke.

"The sahib is a *bahadur*[1] to talk to a man in that fashion, when he knoweth he hath all the soldiers and the government behind him, and my *peshkoza*[2] hath been taken from me. But let him say thus and a quarter thus across the border and I would have disembowelled him—so! I was not fighting, sahib, but thou shalt hear what I was doing. The sentries of thy soldiery move like elephants, and there is little gain in fighting. Only fools fight, and when thy fools were fighting our fools, I and my sons, were sleeping. But at night, when thy sentries are as sheep grazing, we took their rifles. I pray Allah that once more they will soon be fighting that we may have more of their rifles. Aye! Thou knowest the value of such things across the border, sahib."

The next time I visited Sherif Ali I asked him point blank if I would pass as an Afridi.

[1] Brave man.   [2] Knife.

As usual, he did not answer directly.

"There was the *Lat-sahib* Roose-Keppel,[1] *bahadur* who walked in the city streets unmolested, my son. Thy tongue is softer than his. But if thou art perceived, the Afridi hath some knowledge in the matter of slaying a man. It is not always pleasant."

"Zuh takra sarey yum" (I am a strong, fit man), I told him. "Death is to the weak."

"Shabash! Since thou art so resolved, then go and let thy head be shaved."

I was satisfied then that if necessary I could pass as an Afridi. *Shabash!* (bravo!) was praise indeed.

I decided first of all, however, for my own sake, to try out my newly-acquired tongue in the surrounding countryside, and it was on one of these expeditions that I very nearly came to grief once and for all. I should explain that regulations are very strict along the border, intended for the safety of travellers, about where a man may or may not walk. The limit along the main road is 200 yards either side of a military guard. To pass that is to run the risk of inviting serious trouble. At night you are warned to keep off the roads entirely. After sundown the sentries are posted, armed with ball and buckshot, and with instructions to challenge three times and fire. As you may imagine often enough the soldier,

---

[1] Formerly D.C. of Peshawar and afterward, I believe, Chief of the India Office in the War.

his nerves a bit on edge, sees something move, shoots home the bolt and fires immediately on the principle of better safe than sorry!

I was out one day, beyond British India, in the patch of country I described called Yagastan, walking contentedly towards a small village. I was, of course, unarmed—firearms are forbidden—but I had taken the precaution to equip myself with a blackjack improvised from a billiard-cue handle, drilled and loaded with lead. Quite suddenly a figure appeared right in my path, a man I had not seen approaching. I concluded that he, too, was unarmed in that part of the country, when he made a dive into his rags and there he was pointing an ancient sort of blunder-buss at me! It would have been comic if it hadn't been dangerous, and without more ado he let drive at me from his hip and caught me in my left shoulder and chest. If it had been a rifle I should have got mine that time. I went down, but managed to struggle up as he started to run. Something must have scared him, I suppose. As luck would have it, he tripped and I struck at his head without taking any chances. There was a nasty dent in his skull after that and he went right out. He was unlucky and yet lucky. It was the fasting month of Ramazan and I daresay he was an ignorant fanatic who imagined he was earning his ticket to Paradise by sending an infidel to hell. It was unlucky, therefore, I didn't die. Lucky, though, that he did because the British

were quite near, and had I succumbed he would
undoubtedly have been hanged, and the last act of the
hangman to Mahommedan malefactors is to smear
them with pig-fat, which effectually removes all
chance of their entry to Paradise! The horror in
which this degradation is held by Moslems has to
be seen to be believed. I have seen men spit for five
minutes after inadvertently mentioning the very word
khakjeer (pig). I landed up in hospital for a couple
of months after that and on my release I was hauled
before the police and severely censured for being
up there.

However, I didn't care much. I was getting
acquainted with the people, which was what I wanted.

Another thing I did to gain experience was to
obtain permission to go into the lines of the Khyber
Militia. As I had a number of friends among the
civil and military population in Peshawar I was able
to obtain permission to do this from the Commandant. Men in the Militia come from all the border
clans and it was very good linguistic practice for me.
Apart from that I made some very good friends
among them, and they were always courteous and
hospitable to me. They used to tell me what was
happening in the native city, little dreaming, of
course, that I knew as well as they, and I felt sorry
to have to deceive them. A few of their native officers
asked me once if I would care to go with them to the
theatre in the City, and I accepted the invitation.

A trap appeared shortly afterwards with a fine blood horse between the shafts, and I climbed in with the owner and two officers sat at the back. Across my friend's knee lay the largest automatic I'd ever seen, his right hand on the grip outside the holster, reins in his left, evidently ready for trouble!

Everyone of these men have a dozen blood-feuds against them from friends and relations of those they have killed. Hence the swift horse and the gun.

We drove into the city and pulled up as a man appeared and caught the horse's head. I glanced round to find that we were apparently surrounded by about a dozen men who had suddenly presented themselves from nowhere. We got down and, to my intense relief, I discovered that this was our own escort!

My idea in going to all this trouble was an idea which had been forming in my mind for some time past. I had already convinced myself that my enquiries into the question of arms on the other side of the border must be practical to be of any use. I might wait years in Peshawar without finding out a thing of any real value, since apart from a natural reticence on any subject—my attempts at conversation were often received with a non-committal grunt—the slightest reference to rifles was met with complete silence. No one had ever heard of them, apparently. And yet I knew that right under my nose traffic

i

in arms was going on daily. I remembered, too, what
Haynes had told me in Bombay. There was nothing
for it, then, but to go over the border myself and try
to get to Kabul for personal investigation. The
difficulty was how?

I suppose I should have had more respect for
British military vigilance than to make my first
attempt. However, it seemed the simplest method
and I tried it. From time to time parties of tourists
drove up in two-horse gharries from the cantonment
to Ali Musjid beyond Jamrud at the entrance of the
Khyber (about eleven miles), and I duly enrolled
myself in one of these expeditions, hoping I could
hang about until dark and slip through Ali Musjid
into Afghanistan proper.

It worked beautifully—up to a point. I escaped
from my gharrywallah on a trivial pretext, waited
until nightfall (hiding is a fairly simple matter in
those hills) and made my way along the pass towards
Ali Musjid. I knew that there wasn't much chance
of being picked off by an Afridi sniper until I got
up beyond there, and as the gharry had been paid
my driver would not wait. For a good hour I walked
cautiously along the caravan route until I thought
I was through the last British outpost.

A moment later my hopes were dashed. I must
have been mad anyway to imagine I could get to
Kabul alone and unarmed. Two figures loomed
out of the darkness and challenged me in English.

The Khyber Rifles, of course, doing their job properly. Gently but firmly I was led back to the station at Jamrud where I had to explain my 'misfortune' to the officer in charge. I had got separated from the party accidentally and was lost, wandering in the wrong direction. I don't think he was very convinced by my story, but after informing me that it was not unusual for sentries to shoot on sight up there, and that if I valued my life I'd better not get 'lost' again, he let me go when I had given him my address and identified myself.

So Kabul was evidently not to be reached that way! But, as always before in my life, the forbidden fruit looked more tempting for being seemingly unattainable. I racked my brains for some method of defeating the net which the British have thrown across the mouth of the Khyber, and at last the most obvious ruse occurred to me. If I had entered the Forbidden City as a European, I would leave it an Afridi. I was far better equipped now that I spoke Pushtu and on the word of Sherif Ali could pass with safety as a native. I made up my mind immediately to put my plan into execution. Twice a week the caravans came down from the hills and twice a week the Khyber was opened to let them pass out. The purchase of a beast and perhaps a few goods to carry back presented no difficulty to me. I was in any case a bona-fide merchant. The idea seemed good.

A week later I was back in the house of Sherif Ali and confided my plans to him. He shook his head gravely when I told him.

"How can a man avoid the fate that Allah has written for him?" he said. "May Azrael pass thee by, my son."

I knew by this that he felt I was taking a big risk. However, I was aware of that myself, and now my mind was made up nothing could deter me. I had two days in which to prepare myself and these I spent in purchasing a donkey, food, and a few lengths of silk.

I should explain here that in the interval of my acquiring Pushtu and my attempt to get to Kabul I had embraced the Mahommedan faith. As the reader will believe, religion in the sense I knew it had never affected me very deeply. I associated it chiefly with prayer-meetings, salvationists and the come-to-glory brothers of the Western world. It was therefore in no sense a conversion. After I had talked of religion with some of my Indian friends, I went as much on impulse as anything else to a wise old mullah, a friend of Sherif Ali, who explained to me the Moslem philosophy of life and code of behaviour. He didn't ask me to "come", but simply if I thought them good. I spoke with him several times on this, and was eventually accepted as a member of the faith and a follower of the Law of the Prophet. And despite what may appear a rather violent life, tinged with the blood of men at times, I still consider myself a Moslem. There is no good Moslem. Either you are a true believer, or an infidel. Most of the men I have helped out of this world I think have, by their death, made it a better place.

Be that as it may, I think it was this act of mine which sealed the bond of friendship between myself and old Sherif Ali. We had long passed the stage of being merely business associates. He was my teacher, and I knew trusted me implicitly. In any case, in my delicate position my life was always in his hands in Peshawar City where as a *feringhee* a word to any man would be enough to cause my mysterious disappearance. Although I called him "Father" and he "my son" yet we were brothers. Not long after my arrival we were talking when perhaps some word or gesture caused him to ask me: "How old is your mother?" I nearly jumped out of my skin. Carefully and guardedly I answered him. I helped him spell the word. From that moment I knew we were both members of a universal brotherhood. I knew I could expect every assistance from him, however dangerous or foolhardy he might deem my plans.

The night before my departure Sherif Ali decided that a little entertainment might not be amiss (considering, perhaps, that this was the last he would ever see of me!), and after the evening meal we retired to the flat roof with one or two of his friends to smoke hubble-bubbles and watch the dancing girls. This was a fairly usual and not particularly exciting form of amusement which I had experienced several times previously and I only mention it here as it had a sequel later.

We lay on rugs and charpoys listening unemotionally to the insistent rhythm of the hand-beaten tom-tom as one girl after another swayed sensuously before us, performing dances each movement of which I knew was meticulously accurate and probably a thousand years old.

They were young girls mostly, destined later for "The Street of the Harlots" perhaps, lithe, supple, sometimes almost beautiful. The last girl to appear struck me in an odd and unaccountable way as distinct from the rest. Her skin was exceptionally light, her features small and refined, but otherwise there was nothing special to distinguish her from the rest of the girls we had already seen. However, she interested me sufficiently to call her over.

"What name hast thou?" I asked her.

"They call me Noor Jehan,"[1] she answered laughing. "Thinkest thou that I dance well?"

"Well enough," I told her, and threw her a few coins.

"May the light shine upon thy face, my father."

[1] Light of the World.

I waved her away, little dreaming that I was to see her again four years later.

At dawn the city gates opened and I merged myself into the lengthening string of loaded camels, donkeys, chattering merchants, dogs, women and babies. To all who asked I was Yusuf Khan, an Afridi trader of the Zakka Khel. As we moved slowly out of the city up toward the pass, I looked round wondering when I should next see Peshawar City. If I was caught, it might be in a few hours. If not——

At Jamrud we were halted in the *serai*, a hundred or so beasts and as many men, and a detachment of Khyber Rifles thrust their bayonets through the bundles searching for smuggled arms. No questions were asked and in silence guns and knives were returned to those who had been obliged to deliver them up on the way down from Afghanistan. It is an inflexible rule of the British authorities that no armed man comes through the Khyber. The need for personal protection is supposed to vanish once a man is in British India, and the use for any other purpose is strongly discouraged!

When the business was done we filed slowly out again up the long wind into the Sulimans and into the Pass. Another thirteen miles and we had passed Ali Musjid and—*I was through!* Nothing short of death from the bullet of a sniping raider could stop me now from reaching my objective, for I was not afraid of being detected by any of my fellow merchants. We spoke little enough, moving slowly forward until nightfall, when each man looked to himself for food and company. As far as I remember the sole interesting piece of information I gleaned on that long walk was how a man might bring money safely along the caravan route from Kabul to the Pass. If it became known (and news travels quickly up there) that he was carrying any silver rupees a man's life was not safe even from the depredations of his fellow-travellers. He might well have his throat cut one night for the sake of a few rupees. The usual ruse, therefore, was to empty the stomach before departure and *swallow the money*, starving *en route* until it could be evacuated in Peshawar. I cannot vouch for the truth of this unsavoury story other than the fact that I heard it told by a man who had been obliged to do it, but it is fairly illustrative of the difficulties of doing any sort of business other than trade by barter in a country where safe conduct is anything but assured.

The rest of the 160 mile journey to Kabul was accomplished quite easily and, I gathered, unusually safely, since along the whole of the route only one loss was reported. A camel disappeared mysteriously one night, and rather than risk his own life looking for it, the owner evidently decided to cut his losses and trudged dejectedly back with the rest of the caravan, assured that Allah had willed it and he must pray that he might do better next time.

As we approached the city the caravan began to disperse gradually, some of the traders and their families returning to their homes in the district, others travelling on through to Turkestan, Samarkand and Bokhara.

I found quarters for myself in one of the bazaars just outside the city, near the Lahori Gate (one of the two which now remain as the only evidence of the old walled city) and, as Yusuf Khan the merchant, proceeded to do a certain amount of legitimate business buying Bokhara rugs. At the same time I was keeping my eyes open (and my mouth shut) for evidence of any activity in the other business which concerned me considerably more.

I found Kabul itself to have been rather over-rated in the descriptions I had been given in the Peshawar cantonment. Although, of course, it was much larger than the native city of Peshawar, the streets were just as narrow, dirty and foul-smelling, and beyond the erection of one or two important buildings, there was little evidence of the 'modernisation' which was supposed to have been instituted by Amir Abdur-Rahman some years before.

My visit I really reckoned a disappointment, as although I had managed to gather a certain number of facts, I saw or heard nothing to support Haynes' stories of fortunes awaiting the white adventurer.

I decided therefore, for the time being at any rate, to stick to my own connexions in India and see what they proposed to make of the facts I could supply. I stayed in Kabul barely three weeks and then joined a caravan once more and made my way back to Peshawar.

CHAPTER IX

GUN-RUNNING!

I

I BEGAN to assemble my information for transmission to Mukerjee. In the first place I had discovered that the Amir really had a small number of white engineers in his arsenal in Kabul, probably Russians, but lack of modern equipment restricted the potential output to under 20,000 cartridges per diem and the number of rifles was barely 75 per week. This was further complicated by the fact that there was no standard type of rifle, several patterns being used and, of course, cartridges of different calibre. This was not nearly enough for the demands of his own 'regular' army, quite apart from the rest of the male population which did not consider a man worth his salt unless he was the possessor of at least one rifle and a marksman's eye with it. In consequence the Lee-Enfield British service magazine rifle, or a modern Mauser was worth a good deal of money. Among certain border tribes the price had risen to the equivalent *weight* in silver rupees, and was certainly never less than Rs. 800 apiece.

Most of the manufactured arms from Europe, whole or in parts for assembling, were run into Bushire in the Persian Gulf and brought thence to Kabul by camel. As this had to be done carefully to avoid any seizure *en route* by marauding tribesmen, it was a hazardous undertaking, and all travelling was done at night. However, there was undoubtedly money in it for anyone who got through—a profit of a good few hundred per cent, and I wrote to Mukerjee that if he thought it worth while financing, I would take the risk.

The only reply was a summons, sent through Sherif Ali, to return to Bombay immediately, which I did, wondering whether my little scheme had appealed to my employer.

After establishing myself at the Taj Mahal Hotel I went straight to his office where we immediately began to discuss my various consignments and how I had acted in Peshawar. No word of the other matter was breathed until that evening when I went round to his house on the Malabar Hill for dinner. When we had eaten an excellent meal he drew me aside and said in English: "I was very interested in your letter from Peshawar, and I must thank you for going to such lengths to collect your data. I'm not sure, though, that a journey to Bushire and back to Kabul won't be too risky an affair if we are going to buy in any quantity. Have you any notion of the price this material fetches at the port?"

I told him, and he began to make calculations on
a piece of paper. At length he looked up, and still
addressing me in English, said: "If you care to make
a little more for yourself, I have another idea. It
will mean a trip to Europe."

I suppose my expression must have betrayed my
utter surprise, for he laughed and went on: "While
you have been away I have had certain information
from other sources respecting the price at which
these goods can be purchased at the fountain-head.
Now I have a proposition to make."

I do not propose here to acquaint the reader
with just what terms he made me to carry out his
plan, but will merely state that his suggestions
were more than generous and I accepted them
instantly.

"Very well, then," he concluded, "in ten days'
time you will take a boat from Karachi to Bushire
assuming your identity as an up-country Pathan. I
will arrange that you pick up money there—it is
inviting suicide to carry it with you—and you must
then get in touch with the officer of the boat which
runs in the next consignment and arrange a passage
to Hamburg with him. Reaching there, you will
communicate with an address I shall give you, and
effect a meeting with an individual whose name I
shall also give you. He is in a position to supply
you with all the goods we can safely negotiate between
Bushire and Kabul. I leave it to you to arrange the

freightage and, of course, you will travel back with
the consignment."

After he had said this, we immediately changed
the subject and reverted to speech in Hindustani.
I was not a great deal wiser for what he had told me,
and certainly no eavesdropper could have realised
what on earth we were talking about. It was another
example of the veil of secrecy with which all things
are shrouded in India and I knew it was not until
the last minute before I sailed that he would give
me any definite names and places.

I was pretty pleased with the idea, not alone
because it would be my first trip to Europe, but
because the financial inducement was extremely
inviting. Also I was flattered to see how implicitly
Mukerjee trusted me. But I had given my word and
now that I had become a Muslim, I realised that the
hand of every other Muslim in the world would be
against me if I was "not true to my salt"—*nimuk
halal*. In that respect Mahommedanism is one vast
brotherhood—a sort of freemasonry, and if the true
believer fails he is cast out to become a pariah among
men. Sometimes an even worse fate awaits him. . . .

For the next ten days I was largely occupied in
preparing myself for my journey. I had already a
pretty shrewd idea that guns were not run into
Bushire itself—the Anglo-Persian Oil Company had
already made the place a hive of British officialdom
and as far as I knew the freighter lay a couple of

miles off the port itself, and that to avoid the excise patrols the arms were put in at night by row-boat to a cove about ten miles north of Bushire near a collection of fishermen's huts called Khor. All this, of course, was not even hearsay; it was for the most part conclusions I had drawn from conversation concerning (apparently) something entirely different. It would all need careful confirmation, and until I reached Bushire I was completely fogged as to how to go about it. Mukerjee afforded no assistance and I doubt whether he knew, either. People who are directly concerned with the practical end of gun-running are apt to find a little knowledge a dangerous thing. It was far safer, from his own point of view, that he should remain in ignorance.

I saw Haynes, the I.C.S. man, once or twice before I left, and he asked me how I had got on up in the North. I did not dare to tell him of my experiences, although I do not think he would have been anything but highly amused. He asked me if the tribesmen were still up to their tricks gun-pinching, and I was able to satisfy his curiosity with a number of tales which had been the talk of European Peshawar while I was up there. Almost every day horses would mysteriously disappear from locked stables, soldiers sleeping in barracks locked and guarded would miss their rifles in the morning, and a certain major sleeping under canvas in the compound of his bungalow with two sentries posted had woken one morning to find himself staring at the sky. Tent, mosquito nets, clothes and equipment had disappeared into thin air overnight! The father of cunning, the Afridi, had been at work again while he slept.

Before we parted Haynes said to me: "Mac, when I leave the Service, I'm damned if I don't have a crack at getting to Kabul. If they need guns all that bad, I think I might be useful up there myself."

"Not a bad idea," I told him and wondered what he'd have said if he knew.

II

The trip from Karachi would probably have been a nightmare to most people—in fact to myself a couple of years previously. But I was in Afridi clothing and became myself part and parcel of the throng of natives which lined the decks of the vessels going up the gulf.

The night before I left Bombay, Mukerjee had told me that I should find what I wanted at the house of a certain Ya'qub ul Hamdani, a merchant of silks in Bushire. After that, all arrangements were left to myself. Just how much money he had forwarded I did not know, and it was out of the question to ask. I had to wait and see. The name of my assignation in Hamburg also awaited me there. The likelihood of any 'trouble' on the boat was therefore

reduced to a minimum as I scarcely knew myself
just what I was going for!

III

On the appointed day I took the train from Bombay
to Karachi—once more as Yusuf Khan, Afridi of
the Zakka Khel.

A rather amusing incident occurred at this point.
I went to the booking office on the station, laid
down the money and asked for my "tikkut" to
Karachi. The smart looking half-caste clerk grabbed
the money and slung me a ticket, not for Karachi
but a couple of stations up the line. He'd thought
to himself that a miserable peasant from the hills
like myself couldn't read, and the balance of the
fare would go into his pocket. He'd probably
done it every day for years. But, of course, he
struck the wrong man at last. I examined his forbears
verbally in some detail, found them all rotten, threw
doubts on his paternity in the well-known Indian
way, and eventually demanded the right "tikkut".
His face was a picture! *And* I got the ticket immediately!

At about this time I was growing more and more
conscious of the fact that by merely changing my
clothes I assumed native identity not in appearance
only but in—how shall I describe it?—actual fact.
My mind seemed to lose track of westernised modes
of thought and standards of value, and become

K

in tune with those of the people among whom I was moving. The metamorphosis was not yet complete, but later I was to lose my identity as Douglas McHardie so thoroughly that even my native tongue was spoken with difficulty.

However, to continue my story, I boarded an old tin can of a gulf steamer, one of those 500 ton boats carrying cargo and a complement of native deck-passengers. There were perhaps forty or fifty of us, and as we arrived on board the Serang of the lascar crew showed us the space allotted to us. On these boats the travelling native is expected to bring and prepare his own food and, of course, we slept on deck.

Each of us carried our clothing and food for the journey tied up in corners, and took turns at cooking in the sheet iron place provided on the deck. Rugs and blankets were spread wherever we could find room, and I settled down to a week's eating, sleeping, cooking and praying all in the same restricted place.

The heat was terrific for those seven days, but if the boat was officered by white men, then surely I could withstand it. Most of us were small merchants, and as is the way with such men in the East, uncommunicative enough about business.

Most of the time in the Arabian Sea we kept in sight of land, though whether this was from nautical consideration or the age and decrepitude of the boat I never discovered, but by the end of a week we had made Bushire in the Persian Gulf, and after we had dropped anchor a mile or so outside in the roadstead, we were rowed ashore by the lascar crew.

Bushire itself I found to be quite a sizable town, but like most eastern cities a maze of narrow, evil-smelling streets, unpaved and dirty, whose only peculiarity in this instance was the fact that all the buildings were of a kind of white coral which I suppose is a local product. I walked to the extremity of the town, eventually discovering Ya'qub ul Hamdani living close to one of the massive round towers which once composed its fortifications on the land side of the city.

He was a little old man with a wispy white beard, whose clothing, though simple, was of fine quality, and I judged him to be an individual of some importance. His rather distant manner changed immediately I mentioned Mukerjee's name, and after we had exchanged the usual courtesies, he invited me to wash and take coffee with him in order to discuss our business at leisure. I explained my mission with some diffidence until he put me at my ease by pointing to the rich rug on which we were sitting and saying: "Such trifles as these are not always earned by selling silk, O, my son. These old eyes have sometimes sought other merchandise."

It was a plain hint that he also was mysteriously 'in the know' and part of the great unorganised 'racket' in which I was now playing a dangerous part.

I pointed out that I wanted to get to Europe if possible on one of the boats which brought the contraband into the Gulf. Where should I seek them and how could I get in contact with one of the officers?

"A boat is expected," he told me, "within three days. I think I shall be able to arrange a meeting with the first officer on the night she arrives. Come to my house at dusk and we shall see what I have arranged. In the meanwhile dost thou desire the money I have received from Bombay to remain here, or wilt thou take it with thee?"

"A stranger in a strange city would be ill-advised to carry such a purse, O, my father," I said. "Grant me the favour of retaining it in thy house until such time as all arrangements are made."

"Even so." The old man smiled. "God be with thee then until dusk in the space of three days when we meet again."

I spent the three days in the city of Bushire endeavouring to learn, from what I thought seemed likely sources, what I could of where the guns were run in and how disposed of. I had heard one story while I was in Afghanistan and was anxious to confirm it on the spot for future use.

The method used was safe enough, although it involved the use of considerable nerve. However, the policing of Eastern ports can scarcely be compared with those of Europe and the States—as we all saw in the exploits of the German cruiser *Emden* in the Great War—and provided you are suitably equipped for emergencies, any skipper with a knowledge of the coast in the Gulf could get away with it. To begin with, the guns were rarely landed in the same place and always at night.

The word would go round when she was expected, and several boatloads run in to a cove some way up the coast from the city, from the ship which lay anchored perhaps five miles out. There were no special consignees. Business was done there and then for cash on the shore. There was never any lack of purchasers waiting there with their camels and Arabs. The transactions would be made and by daybreak they were away into the hills on the start of the long trek to Afghanistan.

After that the ship would sometimes proceed to Bushire—supposedly in ballast—and pick up a legitimate cargo for return to Europe, or sometimes put about and clear for Europe right away.

If any questions were asked there was always plenty of documentary excuse for her presence in the Gulf!

Being a stranger in Bushire and without any introduction to that particular underworld I didn't manage to learn much except my way about the city in those three days, and I was glad enough when the time came for me to call once more upon Ya'qub ul Hamdani.

A young Arab received me whom I took to be a servant. When I announced my name he said gravely: "My master hath a message for thee, Yusuf Khan. Go now to the bazaar and in the shop of the seller of coffee calling himself Ali Ben Sabah thou wilt find what is sought. He prays that thou wilt accept this rug too, and that the All-merciful may lighten thy task."

He handed me a rug folded in a neat package, which I took and thanked him. It contained the money the old man had left for me.

The shop I had to find in the bazaar was easily identifiable by its smell and my arrival was evidently expected, for I was immediately asked to go to an upper room.

Here I found the man I had been wanting. I guessed he was the first officer of the gun-runner, a great bull-necked Heinie, and he rose from the table where he was drinking coffee and saluted me in bad Hindustani which I scarcely understood. He nearly fell over when I said: "I guess we'd better talk English, if you can manage that better."

"You speak Englisch very good?" he asked when he had recovered. I decided I had better take a chance.

"I'm a citizen of the United States," I said.

At that he roared with laughter and shook my hand heartily. "Ach! ploody good for you, Yankee!"

he roared. I told him not to make so much noise or we should attract attention, but it seemed to tickle him so much it was some time before we could get to talk business. I don't think he believed me even then.

He said eventually that he thought he could fix a passage for me if I had the money, but that I must be ready to leave the next morning when he would take me to the boat in the ship's launch. As far as I was concerned the sooner I got away the better and I made arrangements to meet him as he suggested. What he was doing in Bushire itself I never discovered, but in that business you don't ask too many questions.

I decided to mail the bulk of the money through to Hamburg and pick it up on arrival, as I imagined it would reach there by the mail boat some time before we arrived. Most of it was in Bank of India notes, but I had enough rupee silver to pay cash for my passage and see me through emergencies. I was still rather nervous about carrying much money on my person, even on a European-owned boat. Persons of scrupulous honesty don't usually interest themselves in the gun-running game!

I thanked the officer after fixing a meeting place for the morning and left the coffee-merchant for my sleeping quarters further down the bazaar. In spite of his amazement when I was obliged to disclose my identity he had asked nothing of my reasons for going to Hamburg, but I suppose he was used to queer customers and only looked at the money end anyway.

A month later I arrived in Hamburg, with papers in order as a member of the ship's crew, at a cost of rather more than half a first class passage from Bombay on a P. & O. liner.

CHAPTER X

HAMBURG

I

As soon as I had picked up my money and exchanged the bulk of it into German currency I began to get my business done. The name which I had been given by Mukerjee was Theodor Mendelsohn with an address in the Hermannstrasse, and having never been in Hamburg or even Europe before I naturally anticipated some beer-dive on the water-front similar to the places in 'Frisco where I remembered most arrangements for contraband took place. Attired in dungarees and boots from the ship's stores, I found myself the object of some attention as, by general enquiry, I got further from the docks up into what was evidently a superior business quarter. I wondered if after all I had got the wrong address and the long journey had been futile. But Hermannstrasse 74 was what I had written down and Mendelsohn was the name, and sure enough when I reached the entrance of a palatial office building there it was:

T. Mendelsohn u. Sohne
Teppische, Mobeldamask, usw :

The offices were on the third floor.

The last dirty look I got was from the lift man, since, in spite of my clothes, the clerk who answered my summons betrayed no surprise. I circumvented the language difficulty in a moment.

"Herr Mendelsohn?" I said trying to look like a question mark, and seizing the pencil from behind his ear wrote Mukerjee's name and address on a piece of paper and prayed for good luck.

The clerk's face remained devoid of emotion and with a remark which I took to mean "wait a minute" disappeared with the improvised visiting card.

A moment later and I was closeted with the Herr Direktor, a typical bullet-headed German with about three chins and the back of his neck like a concertina. We shook hands and he said:

"You do not speak Cherman, so we speak Englisch. But not too much, hein?" I took this to be a joke and laughed, wondering at the same time if I should have to do a lot of explaining.

"Now then, my friend, you are prepared to pay cash for dese goods?"

I breathed a sigh of relief. It was evident that he had been expecting me (possibly Mukerjee had advised him by mail) and knew the object of my visit.

"Sure," I told him. "Good German marks which I'm carrying with me right here." I tapped the parcel I was holding.

He nodded and went to a file from which he produced a sheet of paper and placed it before me.

"I must haf three days to procure," he said.

I looked at the typewritten figures before me. It was a list of the manufactures of about a dozen small-arms firms with prices marked against each!

"But what about packing and freight?" I asked him. "How do I get them aboard?"

Herr Mendelsohn laughed. "If you will please let me know what ship they are to travel on, I will see to all that. You must make your own terms with the master, but I will guarantee to see them aboard."

"Very well," I replied, "I shall want 1,500 multiple-loading approved-pattern Mausers. How much will that cost?"

He made a rough calculation on the blotter and told me. It amounted to just over £1 apiece. I paid him and he stood up once more.

"You will communicate by letter the name of the ship to which these goods are to be consigned," he snapped. "Good-day, *mein Herr!*"

Never once had he mentioned the word gun, and indeed, for all the excitement he betrayed he might have been talking about barnyard roosters. I didn't like parting with so much money without so much

as a receipt, but I was obliged to presume that
Mukerjee knew that 'cash without documents' was
one of the rules of the game.

I went back to the ship and found the officer with
whom I had arranged my passage.

"When do you return to the Gulf?" I asked
him.

He shook his head. "I cannot tell. Maybe in
vun week, maybe two. If you wish to talk about
it, please to meet me to-night in Schmidt's Weinstube
on the Chemnitzstrasse near the Binnenhafen."

Schmidt's was a place more after my own heart.
Indeed, except for the language it might have been
on the Barbary Coast. It was full of sailors, mostly
three parts drunk, smoke, noise and booze. I saw
my friend sitting with a girl at a table in the corner
and went over to him. He sent the girl away and I
explained what I wanted, only to receive my first
disappointment. The boat I had travelled in from
Bushire was going to be laid up for probably a
month.

"Any suggestions?" I asked.

He shook his head. "I haf heard," he said, "of
one boat leaving at the end of dis veek, but I t'ink
she already has a full cargo. You might ask der
capitan. He iss here now."

He pointed to a grizzled old man sitting by
himself with a large jug of wine in front of him

listening to the girl playing a concertina at the next table.

The mate left me and brought him over into the corner where, after we had been introduced with an exchange of drinks, I was obliged to listen to ten minutes of rapid German.

From the head-shaking and pointing that went on, I guessed my friend was having some difficulty about establishing my bona-fides. It is a well known fact in the 'trade' that you never know when the next man's a Government agent, or a spy from the arms factories.

However, at last the mate turned to me and said: "He'll do it if you can agree a goot price. How many cases are going aboard?"

I told him, and they started in again. Finally the old man turned to me himself and to my surprise in much better English than my friend, the mate, said: "You'll have to get them aboard yourself. I can't undertake to do that as my business is running the ship. We can get them unloaded on shore with the rest, but, of course, you understand I take no responsibility for seizure."

"Sure I understand," I told him, feeling pretty pleased at my good luck. "How much do you want for the job? I'll see they're put aboard."

He mentioned a figure which put the price of the guns up by twenty per cent. But they were cheap even at that, reckoning what price they would

fetch at the other end, and, rather than start dicker-
ing with the chance, he might refuse altogether, I
agreed.

"What's the name of your ship?" I asked him,
when we had shaken on it.

"*Magdeburg*," he said. "She's lying in the India
Hafen now and we expect to sail on Saturday."

I jotted the name down and ordered some more
wine. The three of us got very friendly as the
evening drew on, and after visiting half the sailors'
haunts in Hamburg we adjourned to a café for
breakfast where I wrote a letter to Mendelsohn's
informing them of my arrangements.

Everything was working out very nicely, as the
Saturday the *Madeburg* was due to sail gave one
clear day over the three that Mendelsohn required
to procure what he termed 'the goods'. I imagine,
of course, that he was only an intermediary. Where
the guns came from and how they were procured
to sell at that price I don't know to this day. There
is necessarily so much secretiveness about those sort
of undertakings that production and disposal units
act quite independently and their identity is never
revealed to each other, all business being done
through a third party who is obliged to keep his
mouth shut for fear of 'reprisals' from either end.

I went aboard a few hours before the boat sailed
and found to my regret I had missed witnessing
her cargo loaded. I saw the manifest later and was

amused to discover that we were carrying bicycle parts! For the Shah of Persia's Cavalry, I suppose!

The voyage out was uneventful enough, the *Madeburg* being a vessel of about 3,000 tons burthen not unlike the one which had brought me from Bushire, and the only excitement I remember was wondering whether our cargo of 'bicycles' would blow up in the Red Sea, where the temperature turned our iron plates into what felt like molten metal.

Nothing untoward occurred, however, and as we neared our destination the old familiar smells and occasional glimpses of the coast made me glad enough that I should soon be back in the type of country I had come to regard as my own. The brief interlude of a European city with tall buildings and hard-paved streets had brought me no sort of nostalgia for a return to 'civilisation' or Occidental living. I felt positively strange and out of place, and longed to be once more among the tall, guttural-spoken peoples of the hills.

At dawn one morning I heard the engines stop and the anchor cable run out. We had arrived. I went on deck to discover that we were still out of sight of land and I concluded that there we were likely to remain and the cargo would be brought off that night in boats, as usual. I had arranged with the skipper to go ashore into Bushire with the first officer at the earliest opportunity so that I could make arrangements about a convoy of camels and a guide, although I guessed the latter would not be necessary since my own shipment would be run in with the rest of the stuff sold on shore and form part of the general caravan right across Persia and Afghanistan. Accordingly I dumped my clothes— dungarees, shirt, boots and socks—over the side with a certain thankfulness and assumed my identity once more as the Afridi Yusuf Khan.

When we parted on the quay after I had given the officer my thanks, I spoke my last word of English for nearly five years. The stench, the heat, the sand, the cruelty of the Northern Hills of India was in my blood and under my skin again until it became part of me.

CHAPTER XI

ACROSS THE ROOF OF THE WORLD

I

FIFTEEN HUNDRED guns meant thirty camels to be bought and driven to the point on the coast about sixteen miles to the north-west of the city, where I knew the boatload would be run in at dead of night. The average palang load of a good camel is between four and five hundred pounds, but loading to capacity is inadvisable when there is a fair chance of losing one or more by sickness or theft on a journey of about fifteen hundred miles!

I had to act quickly if I was to get there in time. I knew I need not worry about Arabs for drovers or guides since the word would have gone round among those concerned some time before and there were always a number waiting to offer their services to prospective purchasers at the point of departure. But there were provisions to be bought as well, blankets, food and all the accompaniments to a long journey across mountains and desert.

It was pretty tough going the whole of that day and when at the end of it all, in a maze of camels

(I managed to buy a number of the famous Khorassan Long-hairs), blankets, food, heat, dust and stench, I left the city, I had made up my mind that I was going to ride. On my previous excursions with caravans, you will remember I had never essayed the difficult task of camel-riding, having always walked alongside in the usual fashion. However, tired as I was, I felt I could endure any discomfort rather than a swift sixteen mile trek which I knew would be followed immediately by a forced march into the hills before dawn with our contraband.

Unfortunately, however, I omitted the preliminary precaution of binding my stomach with a *pugri* before mounting, and it was not until the Arab I had picked up to help drive the beasts noticed my distress that this was remedied and I made the rest of the trip feeling a little easier. Until this was done I really felt as if my insides were being painfully removed. That was my first experience with the camel as a beast of burden. When I came to know him better I had still less admiration for him. I more stupid beast would be hard to find, which I suppose is not surprising seeing his skull's so thick it can turn a ·45 bullet.

When we arrived, it was well after nightfall and I was amazed at the scene which presented itself. In the darkness a crowd of white-clad figures was gathered on the fore-shore—there must have been fifty or sixty men besides myself—moving about conversing in low tones. Some way behind them I could just discern the shapes of the camels which were to form the caravan, lying motionless and silent. I sent my boy to see to the beasts and joined the other 'merchants'. The boats, it seemed, were late, and there was a good deal of apprehension as to whether the right information had been received. I was able to correct this impression, of course, having travelled with the cargo myself, but it seemed that unless things began to happen fairly soon it would be too late as a certain point had to be reached by daybreak which would put us out of harm's way in the form of detection by the Persian authorities.

After about half an hour, however, a light winking for a split second some way out at sea assured us that all was well, and immediately a movement took place to get the camels prepared to receive the purchases.

Having been to some trouble to do my own buying in Europe I was naturally not concerned with any haggling which might take place before our departure, but I was surprised to notice, for the one and only time I was in the East, that these transactions for arms took place without any of the bartering which is such a necessary feature of any sort of negotiation out there. It was done in this way. The boats put in, each in charge of a white officer who announced the price per case of whatever he was carrying. Mausers, like my own shipment, Lee-Enfields, Martinis, or sometimes just *'jezail'*, guns of old pattern and calibre, which nevertheless find a ready market among the raiders of the hills. Ammunition was rarely bought, although unloaded cartridge cases could always find a buyer. The price fluctuated on each voyage, but was usually a fair one, seeing the risks run, and as time was an essential factor in the whole business, it was 'take or leave it'. Those who felt there was a worth-while profit took what they wanted, while the others waited patiently until the next consignment perhaps two or three months later, when they might buy at a better price.

In a very short time the camels were loaded, the boats had put back and the beach was innocent and deserted. Buyers, guns, camels and Arab guides had vanished into the hills. It was, as I say, the only example I even encountered of efficient business methods in the East.

By dawn we had crossed the Khist River and were in the hills outside Kazerun. We lay there all day, and in fact practically the whole of the journey moved only during the night, especially as we got further from the coast into the interior where any sort of policing or judicial administration only exists in the form of the annual tax gathering. It was the strangest journey I have ever made, avoiding even the smallest villages in case word should be spread that a caravan was on the move and some band of professional marauders smell easy money. Occasionally parties would be sent forward to procure water or a few sheep for food while we slept during the day, every man taking a few hours turn to keep watch.

As the long procession moved forward at nightfall occasionally a shot would ring out and a camel fall. The caravan did not halt. The beast was left there—sometimes with its owner, since if we stopped we might discover the marksman to be a member of a large party and the whole caravan would be annihilated. As it was, one would be picked off from time to time—I counted eight between Bushire and Kabul, although there may have been more. Each member of the caravan remained as an independent unit and there was never a check-up on numbers. We travelled together in silence, only conversing with neighbours when there was food to be found or water to be bought.

Our way lay through the mountains for the most part, across the great desert called Dasht-i-Lut (which itself lies at a great height) dropping only when we came to the vast tracts of salt-marsh and swamp formed by rivers with no outlet. Half the time I did not know where we were or in what direction we were travelling; I became, as day monotonously followed day, a little more inured to the intense cold at night in the hills, especially as

I had managed to procure at one village an evil-
smelling *abba*, a voluminous cloak made of camel-
hair, which despite its age and former ownership, I
found very welcome on the march. But it was only
when I heard the name Sabzawar mentioned that
I knew we must be once again in Afghan territory.
Before we reached the outskirts of Kabul we had
been on the road ninety-seven days!

II

Some hours before we reached the city business
began. Our arrival had been anticipated in certain
quarters, I suppose, and invisible look-out men
posted along the route had borne tidings to the
villages and the city of our approach.

Instead, as was usual with caravans of other commodities, of halting at one of the serais on the outskirts
of Kabul and setting about business in an orderly
fashion, a number of hill-men and city merchants
joined us hours before and 'the market' opened *en
route*.

A white-bearded old man walked along beside me
for some time before I realised that he was going
to make me an offer. After we had exchanged the
usual pleasantries he said:

"That she-camel" (pointing to one of my beasts)
"she is old and broken-kneed; this is undoubtedly
her last journey. For how much dost thou value her
and her load?"

I told him twice what I wanted and we began to haggle.

"Dost thou think that I have here a load of useless *jezail*, fit only for children and the smith's hammer?" I asked him. "The sword of Azrael himself can strike death with no more certainty than these rifles for which I have risked my life."

"Aye," he nodded and continued to walk beside me in silence. At length he asked again to examine the one which I had been carrying on the journey for my own purposes. He appraised it with the eye of an expert and announced that although it would mean starvation to his wife and children, since even that fact would not soften my heart, it was Allah's will that I should be paid five hundred rupees apiece for the load, provided I would include the '*oont*' which, although worthless, might have sufficient hair on her to make the sleeve of a small coat.

And so it went on. By the time we had reached the city I had disposed of my shipment at a very handsome profit.

Out of this I procured for myself a house outside the city, where I soon became known as "a buyer of rugs", and then turned my thoughts towards again communicating with Mukerjee (who, of course, had not heard of me directly since my departure from Bombay), and informing him of the results of our enterprise.

A month later I was back in Bombay once more. I had by now drawn so completely apart from all my western associations that even the idea of assuming European clothes was absolutely repulsive and I made no attempt to do so, nor while I was in the city did I attempt to renew any of the acquaintanceships I had made as Douglas McHardie. As I have explained elsewhere I was Yusuf Khan as much in mind as in speech and appearance.

I gave Mukerjee some account of my activities since we had parted and he seemed amazed to think that I was still alive. I also told him that I had installed myself permanently in Kabul and that now I had my own resources I was going to continue making the Bushire-Kabul run with as much as I could afford to buy when the stuff came off the boats. I did not contemplate another trip to Europe, since if I was acting independently the loss of time would not counterbalance the profit I could make with a limited capital.

He agreed with my suggestion and told me that whenever I found that aspect of 'business' quiet, I had *carte blanche* to act as his agent in the north, making purchases on the same arrangement as we had had before. For some reason he would not disclose he had washed his hands for the moment of any further activity connected with arms smuggling. For a man in his established position, it was (apart from the physical element) a great deal more dangerous for him than for myself. I thanked him for what he had done for me and left for Karachi once more, this time on my own initiative.

That was the first of four trips I made like this, Kabul-Karachi-Bushire-Kabul, picking up guns at Bushire and selling them at a substantial profit at the other end. I do not propose to plague the reader with descriptions of these journeys since even if they were hazardous at all times, I always managed to escape with my life. Only once did I come near to losing it, when we were attacked on the Persian-Afghanistan border by a body of tribesmen. We had just got on to the move after lying up all day, when we were surprised by a fusillade of shots which put four of our camels down and the man in front of me coughed his life out with a bullet in the lungs. I had only a vague idea as to the direction from which we were being attacked, as no one was visible, but I unslung my rifle and got down behind my kneeling camel, praying I was facing in the right direction. All at once I caught the silhouette of a horseman for a moment against the sky a few hundred yards from us. I shifted my position slightly so as to face him. We might, of course, be surrounded, in which case there was small hope for any of us with the valuable burden we were carrying. The caravan had come to a ragged halt this time, the leader presumably sensing that this was no solitary raider. After what seemed an age of waiting for the concerted rush I judged would be made, the air was suddenly rent with a series of sharp reports, not, apparently, directed at us all. A few shouts echoed down to us, and further rifle-shots. As far as we could tell the raiders had themselves been raided!

Either it was the settlement of a blood-feud, or else some neighbouring tribe had got wind of our attackers' intention and were carrying out a somewhat premature attempt to 'hi-jack' them. In any case the front of the caravan evidently realised what was happening and we goaded our beasts into a swift run. For over an hour we left the caravan route and made swift and tortuous progress through the rocky foothill country. Fortunately we saw no more of our pursuers. The two bands had probably succeeded in annihilating each other.

Apart from such incidents as these I pursued the normal life of a peaceful Kabuli merchant, occupying my time between these long trips with a certain amount of legitimate general trading, chiefly in Bokhara rugs. On several occasions I went down into Peshawar city, scarcely remembering the time when I had first made the journey in fear and trepidation. Everything seemed to be going well. I was making money, the life suited me, my whole personality seemed to have changed and I had lost all desire to return to so-called civilisation. I had begun to think it would last indefinitely until one day something happened which was to throw my whole life out of gear again.

One morning, in one of the principal bazaars inside the city I was suddenly set upon by half a dozen men and man-handled into unconsciousness!

CHAPTER XII

IN CHAINS

I

WHEN I came to, I found myself lying on the roadside at the city which I recognised as about a mile away, my clothes torn to shreds and soaked with my own blood. I tried painfully to move, only to feel that something heavy seemed to be weighing down my legs. When I at last manœuvred myself into a sitting position I saw my ankles were shackled with about two hundred pounds of iron-linked chains!

I had often seen notorious criminals and malefactors thus publicly 'imprisoned' along the roadside during my stay in Kabul, but it had certainly never entered my head that I should ever be in that position myself. I was pretty sure I should die, and prayed that it might be soon. To become one of those wretches whose only sign of life was a mass of festering sores and a pitiful mumble for water, was worse than any death. My mind groped blindly for some reason which could have placed me in such a position. I could think of nothing I had done which would have merited this sort of punishment, which was usually reserved for aggravated cases of wrong-doing. A small begging-bowl had been placed at my side, and with that I was supposed to support such life as was left in me for as long as I felt it worth while. Presently, the dogs would come and eat me. . . .

In addition to this revolting prospect I felt horribly ill. Whoever my assailants had been had given me a beating within an inch of my life, and I wondered if I had a sound bone left in my body. Worse than that, I had a raging thirst. How long I had lain there insensible I don't know, for I had been attacked in the morning, and yet judging from the sun, it was not yet midday. I supposed it was the day after.

The instinct of self-preservation was still strong enough in me to make me moan feebly to passers-by.

"Water for the love of Allah! Water in God's name!" I had heard that cry often enough. It is one no true believer may refuse, even to his deadliest enemy.

My swollen tongue would hardly articulate any more when at last a *bhistie* (water carrier) with his goatskin water bag slung over his back came along. I drank greedily, which I suppose was a foolish thing to do, for either I became unconscious again or went into delirium. At all events I remember little more until I was again crying repeatedly:

"Water! Food! Allah have mercy on all givers! Food for the love of the All-merciful!"

Day followed day interminably. I suffered agonies from the heat of the burning sun, only to endure worse torture from intense cold at night. How I kept alive, I do not know to this day. My diet (of such scraps as were thrown to me and the water I begged) began to shew itself in horrible rashes and sores on my body. I became so enfeebled that I could no longer drag the weight of my shackles a few yards to change my position, and for long spells I seemed to remember nothing. I suppose I should be thankful that my lucid moments were few enough in which to reflect on my miserable fate. There was no single person to whom I could appeal, while I did not even know the crime I was supposed to have committed which merited this inhuman treatment. Compared with this a prison would have been the height of luxury!

In spite of my filthy condition—or perhaps because of it—I excited little enough attention from passers-by. I must have presented a revolting spectacle. My torn rags had left me all but naked, my body emaciated to a skeleton and covered with festers, while the whole of my face and head was a mass of filthy matted hair. During that time I believe I was scarcely alive. I can recall none of my thoughts, hardly any of my feelings. Yet in some strange manner the feeble spark of life refused to flicker out. I can only suppose that I must, at the time I was assaulted and flung out on the roadside, have possessed a constitution a little harder than iron.

I was even more astonished when I discovered later that I had been lying there for over eight months!

My wretched plight was at last terminated in a strange manner. There was no hair-breadth escape or good samaritan rescue about it. I was released eventually by personal intercession with the Amir himself!

II

In case the reader should consider that to sound a little too grandiose to be possible, let me explain the circumstances.

One morning, when I had long ceased to imagine that I should ever be freed of my gyves, a party of horsemen appeared along the road—evidently persons of some importance since a detachment of soldiers was following at a discreet distance. I was not particularly curious—curiosity had long ago died in me—but in accordance with my usual practice I set up my cry of "Food, in the name of the All-Merciful!" hoping perhaps for a small coin, when the party drew rein just opposite me.

One of the horsemen pointed at me and although I could not hear what was being said, it was evident that I had aroused some interest. Thinking perhaps this elevated personage might possibly be a *naib*[1] or a *kazi*[2], I redoubled my wailing and changed the tune a little. I should perhaps explain that nominally all Afghan subjects have the right of appeal to the Amir for trial, and he is supposedly accessible at all times to hear complaints. Knowing this I wailed that I was condemned without trial, that in the name of Allah my case might be brought to the notice of the Great Amir, that the All-Merciful would shower his blessing on those who took pity on a poor believer.

To my surprise my howls took effect. One of the men dismounted and came over to me. I grovelled at his feet crying "*Pa makha de khar*, lord." (May light be upon your face) "Thou hast heard thy servant!"

He looked at me in disgust for a minute and then said:

"Thou sayest thou art condemned without trial?"

"Even so, lord."

"Thou hast cried and the Amir has heard thee, spawn of a dog. Thou shalt be brought before him!"

With my remaining strength I shrieked my blessings upon the beneficent Amir as the cavalcade moved slowly off. It was the Amir himself and his party who had ridden by! The attendant courtier

---

[1] Provincial governor.   [2] District judge.

who had spoken to me I recognised subsequently
when I was brought before the Amir in Durbar.

Sure enough some hours later, two soldiers came
to fetch me into the city. I was slung on an ass,
since my chains were welded on my legs, and taken
into Kabul where I was fed, remaining in custody
for the four days before the Durbar was held. I
realised later that I had probably been part of a
sort of annual round-up of such wretches as myself
so that in theory at least, the idea of the Amir being
supreme judicial head, court of appeal and everything else (except for commercial cases) might be
said to have foundation in fact.

My spirits revived considerably at the prospect of
my release and I felt signs of returning sanity,
although my poor body did not respond so quickly.
My chains were removed on arrival in the city and
it is surprising what a few good meals can do for
something that for months has been only half-alive.
It's psychological, I guess, but at the end of those
four days I began to feel interested in remaining
alive again.

Had I any idea of what the Amir of Afghanistan's
Durbar was like I might have preferred to remain
at the roadside. But I'm getting too far ahead.

This Durbar was not to be held in the Durbar
Hall which adjoins the Palace on the edge of the
city, but in an enclosure on the north-east of the
town beyond the Sherpur Cantonment, and there

M

we were taken under strong military escort. I say we, since there must have been a dozen other pitiful wretches looking very like myself who were taken along at the same time.

Apparently on these occasions it was customary to combine business and pleasure, for before 'cases' were heard and often between them, a sort of gymkhana was in progress. The Amir was seated on a raised and canopied dais (I recognised him from my encounter a few days before) surrounded by khans, sirdars, mullahs and the rest of the various officials who formed the Khilwat, which more or less corresponds to a permanent cabinet. However, as the Amir is an absolute despot, cabinet—or even advisers—is scarcely the correct term, for no member of the council may give advice unless he is expressly asked for it.

Persons awaiting trial, including myself, were assembled in a corner under armed guards, and obliged to witness the day's sport before hearing what their fate might be.

Some distance away, a huge bull elephant was shackled by all four feet to the ground. It was not harnessed and from its loud trumpetings and squeals seemed to be somewhat ill at ease, and I wondered what it was for. I supposed it had some connexion with the sports to be held until I later discovered it had a much more sinister purpose.

The first day of the Durbar only two 'cases'

were heard, but they were eye-openers, to say the least. I had hitherto harboured a vague idea that there might be some sort of justice to be expected even of a country where the whole judicial system is centred in one individual, since, after all, the law was the Law of Islam, which in itself is just and equable. I soon discovered, however, that it was capable of the most horrible misinterpretations.

After a long display of horsemanship the first poor devil of our group was summoned and thrown before the Amir by two soldiers. He was not, it seemed, entitled to speak for himself. He lay there, quivering, while the Amir inquired loudly what he had done. It was the business of a tall, grave-faced official at one side of the dais, whom I took to be some sort of Chief of Police, to announce a list of crimes, real or suspected, after which the Amir would either pronounce sentence directly or put it to the vote among members of the Khilwat.

It was as I witnessed this first case that I realised with horrible suddenness that we were all pre-destined to receive one sentence—to be administered in varying forms.

Death!

But not death by decapitation, or by a rifle bullet, or by hanging. Such methods of execution were evidently too straightforward. The Amir wished to be amused at his Durbar. And so it came about that I was the witness of some of the most fiendish refinements of capital punishment which the mind of man can have devised.

Not only that, but a witness with the certainty that just such a fate was in store for me presently. I soon realised the purpose for which the shackled elephant was required. The huge beast had gone *musth*, and the first man to be condemned was taken over and thrown down in front of it! Out flung the long trunk, seized him, held him; then, with one huge forefoot placed on him, the beast's trunk wound round his body and tore him slowly apart. . . . His screams mingled horribly with the enraged trumpetings of the elephant. In my weakened condition I was physically sick as I watched it. Some loathsome fascination kept my eyes open as I saw the next unfortunate wretch bound by his four limbs to four bent saplings whose tops were pegged into the earth. At a given signal the taut ropes holding them were severed simultaneously and the screaming body disgustingly quartered. . . .

After this edifying spectacle the remainder of us were taken back to the mud-wall 'prison' that night and fed again. My agony of mind and the screams of broken men still echoing in my ears rendered me incapable of either eating or sleeping, and the next day we were taken out once more. On this occasion I was forced to see a man put to death in a huge jar of oil beneath which a brazier was lit and the liquid boiled. In my half-frantic

state I remember being stupidly reminded of Ali
Baba and the Forty Thieves, and I expect I joined
in the laughter with the rest of the company. Even
that day I was not to hear my own fate, although
I received a tiny sop of comfort in seeing one of
the unfortunates go free. It had pleased the Amir
to temper his justice with mercy!

The third day my turn arrived and I was hauled
before the dais as the usual questions were called.
I can hear now as I think of it the slow gutturals
of the voice of the man on the dais.

"*What hath this man done?*"

The words I had heard so often fell on my ears
like a clap of thunder.

"The dog is a *jasoos* (spy), lord. Many men have
brought tales concerning him."

So I was a spy! And that was the first time I
had heard even of what crime I was accused. I
faced the dais and in defiance of all rules shouted
my protest.

"Hear me, merciful prince, as Allah is a witness!
I am no spy but a respectable trader. Spying requires brains which I have not. My house stands
without the city, as many will testify, and I have a
poor business as a merchant of rugs from Bokhara
and the northern cities of Turkestan!"

I rambled on, protesting my innocence until my
mouth was stopped by one of the guards who held
me. As I spoke I saw the Amir lean over and address

one of the company beside him. I supposed they were discussing which of the beastly deaths I had witnessed was bad enough for a *jasoos*. There was a good deal of laughter and at length an official was summoned.

I thought the end had come when at length the Amir spoke in a loud voice, delivering sentence. But I was mistaken.

"Take this fellow," he said, "give him a purse of two hundred rupees and a safe conduct to the Khyber with six men. It is better that his trading be done in the bazaars of Peshawar and Lahore."

I could hardly believe my ears when I heard this. Was this just another piece of exhibition 'mercy' for the benefit of his loyal subjects or was I in fact suspected of spying? I neither knew nor, at that moment, cared, and as I was led away, accompanied by the important person (whom I gathered to be an officer in the Amir's personal bodyguard) back to the city, I merely felt a tremendous sense of relief!

III

The officer who had been detailed at the Durbar himself accompanied me with five mounted men. I was still far too weak to sit a horse without assistance and, in consequence, found myself bound, none too gently, on a stout *yabu*,[1] and jolted and

[1] Native Afghan burden-horse.

bumped along the rough track which led down through Jalalabad to the Khyber.

The officer himself was a tall, hawk-faced Afghan of immense height and proud bearing. I don't think he was any too pleased at having the job of running a jasoos out of the country, although subsequent events shewed that he was going to compensate himself handsomely for it. As we rode slowly through the narrow defiles into the hills I began to wonder, when I was not thinking of how much longer I could bear the discomfort, what sort of reception I should get when I reached the border. I had had about enough, and sick in mind and body as I was, felt that even the prospect of a government prison would not be unwelcome.

After about fifteen miles or so we halted and the officer gruffly ordered me to be untied and set down. I naturally thought we were halting for a rest and food, for which I was duly thankful. However, I was sadly mistaken, once again. Had I been in my right mind I should have realised from my knowledge of Afghan methods, that there was never any intention of giving me safe conduct to the border, far less of handing me two hundred silver rupees.

As they released me I tumbled heavily from the horse to the ground and the soldiers mounted again. The officer turned his horse and, calling over his shoulder for me to find my way to the border myself, prepared to ride off. I yelled as loud as I could that he was a cowardly dog to leave a sick man thus, and that the Amir had ordered that he should give me a purse of rupees anyway. I should have been better advised to let matters rest, for the tone of my insults only resulted in his wheeling once more, and I thought he was going to ride me down. Instead he reined just in front of me and leaning over spat in my face. The thin-lipped mouth cracked into a savage grin.

"Consider thyself lucky," he hissed,—"O misbegotten spawn of spies, may thy father's tomb be defiled—that thou art still alive!"

Then, drawing his sword, he started to belabour me with the flat of the blade. Blood began to flow down my face again, and with my remaining strength I crawled away on all fours into the shelter of a rock. The troop turned about and clattered off in the direction of Kabul once more, leading my horse with them.

I slept for a while in the shade, hoping to recover enough strength to crawl a little further until I should come to a village or possibly meet some wayfarer along the caravan route.

Before nightfall I had reached a point where not far below in a little valley I could see a towered village. A tall Afridi, rifle slung on his shoulder, was driving a flock of sheep and goats towards me up to a higher pasture. I lay still hoping he would pass near enough to hail, although I knew he would be as likely to shoot me as look at me. However, if he saw I was sick, I could rely on some assistance as, short only of a blood-feud enemy, the sick may have sanctuary in any village.

When at length he was near enough to hear my feeble shouts, he unslung his rifle in a flash and I heard the bolt click home. As yet he had not seen me and I waved my arms frantically praying he would not pass. Finally he saw my upraised hand, and evidently deciding I was not carrying a weapon in the other cautiously approached.

"*O, sareya*" (O man), I greeted him. "Behold, I am near to death and without food." He approached and lowering his rifle examined me critically.

"Thou art wounded?" he asked. "Some repayment of a debt, a blood-feud? Is thy tower destroyed?"

"May the Lord Mahomet in Paradise be my witness," I replied, "it is none of these things. I was set upon by the lice-ridden Kabuli soldiers, may their souls rot in hell, and left for dead without reason."

He seemed quite satisfied with this explanation, since the average tribesmen has a hearty contempt for the Amir's army, preferring as many of them do to serve for a period in the native levies of the British on the frontier.

"What is thy name and to what clan dost thou belong?"

Once more I told him. "I am Yusuf Khan and my people are of the Zakka Khel."

"That is good," he replied. "Let us go together."

And so for a time I found sanctuary in the tower of Yacoob Khan. When I arrived I drank deep from the water jar and ate ravenously of the onion and pulse stew which is common fare of the hill-folk. Sanctuary for criminals is a recognised tribal code and I was allowed to dwell in the village as a 'shade-fellow' helping (as soon as I was able) to earn my keep in various ways.

As I gradually regained my strength I began to think once more what I should do. While I lay, sick in mind and body, in the tower of my rescuer, I had plenty of time to reflect on my position, and the events which had led up to it. Spy! I began to revolve in my mind the pretext which might have been used by my accusers for supposing this. While I was innocent enough in intention, was it possible that I had been used unwittingly? Memories came crowding back of my occasional visits to Sherif Ali. He had often asked me, I remembered, quite casually what things I had seen and heard, what rumours were rife in Kabul, had I seen so-and-so. Was it possible that he——? He had seemed uninterested enough in my answers, just grunting between pulls at his pipe—"*Khair dai*" (good) or "*Parwa nishta dai*" (It doesn't matter).

The more I thought of this, the more certain I

became that I had indeed been used as a catspaw in some game of which I had not the remotest knowledge. For generations Afghanistan had been a hive of political intrigue, European and Asiatic, and it was into that net that I had been drawn. It was not only the arms traffic which had interested Sherif Ali.

Once I had established that I had to think out my movements carefully.

I was no longer in any mind to go down across the border, apart from the slight possibility that news of my being sent down to the pass as a spy might conceivably have reached the ears of the British Military Intelligence who would probably be waiting for me. That only meant a further spell of interrogation and imprisonment or deportation. I was living among people I liked (despite their treacherous and savage dispositions they were above all *men*), and in the Afridi country a man can live just as long as he can shoot and use a knife. It was towards the end of my third month in the village that I began to hear mentioned a name which had become familiar to me long before while I was still in Peshawar. *Khaidar Khan!*

He was the leading spirit (there are no acknowledged 'chiefs' among the Afridi, for each man considers himself better than the next) of a band of particularly fearless raiders, who had long been a thorn in the side of the British authorities, and whose feats of daring—always accompanied by pillage, rape and arson—were a byword in all the bazaars of the North West.

The idea took shape in my mind that if I could, I would find this man and offer my services, if they were acceptable, in return for his protection.

CHAPTER XIII

REVENGE AND A BORDER RAID

I

I HAD better acquaint the reader first of all with what I knew of the notorious Khaidar Khan before I actually encountered him. As his name was a byword, naturally the stories I had heard were hearsay, but I later discovered that nearly all of them had some foundation in fact.

"A man among men, a killer among killers!" A *bahadur!* I first remember hearing his name glorified in a bawdy song sung by the women in the courtyards of the Street of the Harlots in Peshawar, and had afterwards elicited some information to satisfy my curiosity about the man. It seemed that he had served for a period, like so many of the men of the hill-tribes, with the British native militia, reaching the rank of havildar. His brother was serving at the same time and had been punished for some misdemeanour which, trifling enough in itself, nevertheless appeared to Khaidar Khan in the light of a deep injustice. So incensed had he become at his brother's treatment that he had taken the very rare step of becoming *nimak harami* (untrue to his salt), and in fact broken his oath and deserted. He had disappeared one night with his rifle and as many rounds of ammunition as he could carry and from that moment had become one of the most troublesome raiders on the border, harrying peaceful communities, burning villages, descending on Peshawar city, stealing rifles and horses from the cantonment, and generally incensing the authorities to such an extent that a price of 5,000 rupees was put on his head, in the hope that one of his followers would be treacherous enough to betray him for the bribe—a not unusual occurrence among men who boast they have but one allegiance and that to themselves. He was a man of the Alum Khel who are well-known for their fighting qualities, and when I eventually saw him, confirmed all reports of his personal appearance. As with the border Pathans generally he was very light-skinned, stood a good six foot six in his bare feet, with a hawk-nosed face of extraordinary ferocity. His skull, which would have been amply covered by a good sized breakfast-cup, contained only two mental attributes. Cunning and cruelty.

Such was the man I had made up my mind to seek out. How I would be received when I found him, and how that was accomplished I did not know. But with an outlaw a man with a grievance may often find himself welcome. I had a grievance—

not against the British but against the dog of a Kabuli officer who had left me for dead. I was determined to settle that score, and in the meanwhile I might find the protection of the notorious Khaidar Khan, to say the least of it, useful.

As soon as I was well enough I left the house of Yacoob Khan and set out to find my objective as best I could. It is not an easy task to locate men of that type in the hills. There is a carefully studied ignorance of their whereabouts which would make it easier (and safer!) to ask where the vultures roost as where Khaidar Khan lay waiting. In the end it happened that I came across him by chance.

One evening toward sundown I was nearing a village intending to pass the night there when I was met by a swarm of yellow pariah dogs—the alarm signal in every hill-village. These great half-starved mongrels roam in packs and at times become ferocious enough to pull a man down. When that happens God help him, for they leave neither hide nor hair! The villagers rely on these scavengers to warn them of the approach of any stranger, as their howling and snapping makes it impossible for anyone to enter the village un-heralded. I beat them off as two men appeared from the direction of the village, rifle in hand.

They inquired in a surly tone my name and business, and I told them I sought only food and drink as I was a lonely traveller. They took me to the centre of the village, where, grouped in a rough circle, sat some twenty or thirty men. They regarded me with unfriendly eyes without rising as I appeared—a most unusual manifestation among men with the Eastern philosophy of hospitality. But the giant who sat among the furthest from me supplied the reason. His immense stature and ugly visage tallied sufficiently with description for me to identify him immediately as the man I had been seeking—Khaidar Khan!

I approached slowly and greeted him:

"*Starra ma shai!* I am Yusuf Khan, a traveller seeking food and drink. Do I not behold the man who's name is on all lips? I, too, am a man who seeks revenge on my enemies."

He waited until I had finished, his eyes boring into me. Then he spoke, gruffly. "I have heard of thee, Yusuf Khan, who were found by the road-side by Yacoob Khan. *Jasoos!* We wish for no spies here. I am minded to give thee to these men for sport!"

There was only one way to treat this sort of talk if I was to succeed in my object. I pulled out my knife and called to him: "Up, man, on thy feet. No man calls me spy while I have my strength. Up, that I may disembowel thee now and use thy gut for my bedstrings!"

He rose halfway to his feet and then fell back again on the charpoy bellowing with laughter.

"Hai!" he yelled, waving a long arm. "Mahommed Khan, Gulab Din, Ahmed Shah, up and give seat to a man. Perhaps presently we will see if his deeds are as good as his words. Let him be with us for the eating and drinking."

As I partook of his hospitality I told him of the indignity I had suffered in Kabul and after. He listened patiently and then asked: "What seek ye with me, O Yusuf Khan?"

"It is told," I replied, "that thou hast men to the number of four hundred at thy call, Khaidar Khan. Do but summon them and come with me and I will shew them where there is money and jewels for the taking, women and perhaps a few men to be sent to Paradise."

He grinned as I spoke and said: "I choose my own fighting, Yusuf Khan. Besides, how shall I trust thee when talk counts for less than nothing. Go first and avenge thyself on this Kabuli of whom you speak so often and who spat upon thee. If thou art such a man as thou pretend, settle first that debt, then return and perhaps then we will travel together."

So that was that. At least I had established contact with this almost mythical figure, and the following morning I left the village with the certainty that I had not seen the last of the notorious Khaidar Khan.

N

II

I went back to Kabul and stayed there for a week, living in the bazaars, only venturing out at night. I revisited my old house outside the city only to find it had been appropriated by the police, or what passed for them, and resold to a family. All the time I kept my eyes open for the officer in the Amir's bodyguard. The chances of seeing him, in spite of the size of the city, were not so small as might appear to anyone who is used to seeking persons in, say, Exeter or Tulsa, Okla. In Kabul there is one certain centre of exchange of information, especially about soldiers and the official class, and that is the stews, the red-lamp houses, the harlots' quarter—call it what you like. It was there that I discovered my quarry's name—Abdul Rahim. He was a personage of some importance, I heard, and a frequent visitor to a certain house of women where young girls were reserved for his attentions exclusively. I was told I should certainly find him eventually if I watched the house.

And so, every night, I made my way through the dimly lighted bazaars and dark, crooked alleys to wait in the shadows for the man I had sworn vengeance upon. For ten days I went there every night praying that when he came, he would come alone.

Then one night I saw him. I could not mistake the man who had spat upon me—the ultimate insult to give to a follower of Islam. He passed a dozen yards from where I stood and went into the house I had been told about. From behind the grilled window apertures came the faint tinkling sounds of the dancing girls. It was almost dawn before he reappeared and I had begun to wonder whether perhaps he had gone from some other door and escaped me. I followed him noiselessly in my grass sandals, a keen-edged *peshkoza* in my hand. There was to be no mistake about it. The man was to die. I don't believe he even recognised me as I caught his shoulder and flung him round to face me. There was a look of surprise on his evil face. The last words he heard were those of the oath I whispered as I struck upward with all my force: "*Haramzada khudai dey bekh obasa, dozakht ta larsha*" (May God tear out your roots).

Abdul Rahim, captain of the Amir's bodyguard, died without a sound, and I left him for the dogs to eat.

Before sunset the following day I was back in the hills and by nightfall had reached the village where Khaidar Khan had his temporary headquarters. As I gained the entrance, a man was squatting outside kneading *chuppatties* by the smoky embers of a little wood fire. He seized the rifle at his side in a flash as he saw me, then, perceiving my own upraised hand and slung weapon, suspiciously challenged me.

I gave my Afridi name which he shouted loudly and permission was given for me to enter. Khaidar Khan was sitting on a string charpoy surrounded by a dozen of his savage looking henchmen—all fellow outlaws.

"Mayst thou never be tired!" I greeted him.

"Thou also, Yusuf Khan," he replied. "What news?"

"The Kabuli pig, may his mother's tomb be fouled by dogs, has gone to join his ancestors in hell," I told him. "Here is a token." I unwrapped from my *pugri* a finger with a gold ring, which won approval in the form of a shout of laughter.

"How shall one escape the will of Allah?" commented Khaidar Khan grimly. "It is a deed well done."

When he had eaten that night, he said to me: "Men say thou knowest well the city of Peshawar, Yusuf Khan?"

I nodded.

"And thou dost desire to live in sanctuary with us as shadefellow?[1] Then thou canst serve by going through the hills to the city to prepare the way for us. Gulab Din shall go with thee, for there his face is not known."

---

[1] Refugees from the law on both sides of the border are often given sanctuary by parties of raiders and earn their keep by exploring the lie of the land preliminary to a raid where the tribesmen might be known and arouse suspicion.

A man came in later that night whom I understood was to be my companion. I gathered from the conversation which ensued that he had just returned from a private arm-procuring expedition outside Peshawar Cantonment. He proudly exhibited a British Service Lee-Enfield of the type I had seen often enough used by sentries. He entertained us for some time with the grisly story of how he stole the gun.

A small force was out in the hills and for hours he had lain in a nullah about twenty yards from where a sentry was posted. When the guard had been changed he lay still watching the solitary figure with the rifle chained to his waist. The sentry had been a kid, it seemed, probably just out from home. ("The hair hath not grown on his chin," was the way he put it) and was looked on as easy meat. After a long time the man who lay in the nullah threw a little pebble to the right of the sentry. In the deadly quiet the sound was immediately perceptible. The boy had started and looked about him. Within ten minutes, the Afridi had thrown another pebble, this time to the left.

Any unexplained sound in that stillness can try a man's nerves, where for all he knows the innocent hills may be alive with hidden cut-throats. The man in the nullah had watched the sentry start again, and peer carefully in the direction of the sound. Plip! A third pebble fell about half-way between them. It had been more than the boy could stand. He had left his post to investigate.

That was all the Afridi wanted. The boy's curiosity was satisfied with a knife-thrust in the back. One hand had stifled his cry. He died quite soundlessly. To secure the chained rifle was merely a matter of severing the belt at the waist.

The method of protection used on such occasions by the British was for the sentries to call their posts at half-hour intervals: "Number one and all's well!" and so on the whole way round. The time would have come when the solitary figure failed to make his call and the sentry would be found dead, lying inexplicably twenty yards from his post. It's quite simple when you hear how it's done, but that sort of thing puzzled the British for years.

To the Afridi it's just a good evening's sport. A decent rifle is worth more than a man's life, especially an Englishman's. . . .

III

A few days later I was on my way back to Peshawar a member of Khaidar Khan's band of killers! His method was not to travel en masse but in groups of five or six with instructions to reach an agreed rendezvous about half a mile from the city walls after dusk.

My party reached the objective, and as daylight broke I saw myself in company with one of the finest collection of cut-throats this side of hell. We had made our way to this point not by the familiar caravan route which runs down through the Khyber but by a difficult route through the hills which I did my best to remember for future use. The procedure decided upon was what I understood to be the usual one in these cases. At daybreak two men were detailed to enter the city to buy food and reconnoitre while the rest remained outside awaiting their return. They came back at last with sufficient food for the return journey, and on their information the plans were laid. Towards late afternoon a party of about ten men, unarmed and posing as ordinary citizens were sent into the city where they again separated arranging to meet near one of the gates at sundown. After giving the rest of the main party outside sufficient time to reach the other side of the gates they were to dispose of the policemen, open the gate and fire two shots as signal.

It worked like clockwork. The gun used for the signal was that of the guard on the gate.

At dusk, down we went and lay concealed, waiting for the signal. At last it came, and up and in we rushed howling like madmen.

I thought I had been in some scraps but that first raid on Peshawar beat them all. We just took everything we could lay hands on. Any sort of resistance was met with a knife-thrust or a rifle bullet. I saw one man disembowel a shopkeeper who had swallowed the key to the room where he kept his money! A lot of the killing was sheer wanton, blood-mad murder. A few carried resin-soaked torches and the lightly built structures of lath and mud soon began to go up in crackling flames to add to the indescribable confusion. At intervals above it all I could hear the bull-like voice of Khaider Khan: "*O sareyan, mala rasha!*" (This way men!) What a shambles was there that night! Men, women and children running in all directions, screaming with terror. The dreaded Khaidar Khan was down from the hills again!

It seemed to go on for hours. I was down by a wall attempting to bind a gash in my thigh I had caught from a butcher's axe as I stepped over a prostrate body, when I heard again that great roar: "*Mala durwaza ta larshae!*" (To the gates with me!) I staggered in that direction and we went out with a rush. There was no policeman to be seen on this one!

It was out and away into the hills again, thirty miles before dawn. Not a man was there who couldn't carry sixty pounds and a rifle that distance. In addition to our precious loot, several girls had been bagged. A brief halt was made after about ten miles to ascertain if they were worth taking further. Being heavily veiled, their ages were uncertain quantities. There were two old women in a total of five. These were promptly despatched with execration and a quick knife-thrust, and we pressed on. It was accounted a highly successful expedition.

I heard later that the troops were called in to fight the fire and blast away a number of houses to prevent it spreading.

Khaidar Khan was highly pleased, and after we had slept, we ate well that day: two lambs were roasted and many a partridge and sweetened curds eaten with them. After that I was accepted. I "belonged".

And so it went on. Occasional raids were made on small villages, perhaps where there was known to reside some rich man, sometimes an individual tower was razed to satisfy a feud or because it contained something worth having. I did not accompany them all, of course, but as time passed I was regarded with less suspicion and eventually came to be accepted with the rest of the hillmen. I had long since ceased to think of myself in any other way. Yusuf Khan the Afridi had entirely ousted what was left of Douglas McHardie the Californian. . . .

CHAPTER XIV

ESCAPE FROM THE GALLOWS!

I

MY association with Khaidar Khan came to an abrupt conclusion. It must have been about eight months after I had first been admitted as one of his gang that another raid on Peshawar city was projected. On this occasion I was selected a member of the advance party as being least likely to arouse suspicion, and a fierce-looking Adam Khel Afridi by the name of Kudar Bux was chosen to accompany me. As the same tactics were to be employed as before, we departed together and entered the city soon after dawn. Word had reached us from the border that as a result of the persistent trouble he was giving, the price on Khaidar Khan's head had been raised by the British authorities to 6,000 rupees. However, this did not seem to worry him in the least, in spite of the fact that, next to revenge, personal gain even at the expense of one's own brother, is a thing for which an Afridi will willingly risk his life.

I was not immediately suspicious when Kudar Bux suggested that we should separate as soon as we got inside the city and meet later at a prearranged spot. There was a woman, he said, and I made no attempt to disagree with his suggestion. But at the same time I knew the British Government House was only a mile outside the city. Once again the main body, with Khaidar Khan himself, lay in the hollow of a dried river-bed about three miles away, waiting for dusk. When the time arrived for my meeting with Kudar Bux I was surprised when he failed to appear. After waiting some time I thought that the best thing to do would be to go back and warn the others that he had disappeared. Something untoward had happened. I had no thought at first of any treachery but as I neared our rendezvous I realised instantly what had occurred.

The son of a dog had sold us out for blood money! A detachment of troops was at that moment already engaged in endeavouring to wipe out Khaidar Khan and his followers, and they succeeded, too, by sheer weight of numbers, although it took them ten hours to do it. In the fighting Khaidar Khan was killed—a better death than hanging in Peshawar Gaol. He was the last man killed—horribly riddled before he finally went down. The coup-de-grace was given by a mounted trooper who used his head as a tent-peg, and drove a lance through his mouth and up through his skull. I saw this with my own eyes! Not more than a dozen men reached the safety of the hills that night. I was taken prisoner with

four others, while the rest lay among the rocks for
the vultures to pick their bones.

We were marched off under a strong guard to the
military gaol in Peshawar cantonment with the
certain prospect of being tried and hanged the next
day. They don't waste any time about those things
up there. . Men of the border tribes have an uncanny
way of disappearing apparently into thin air if they
are left to meditate too long in a prison. The British
thought they were clever, too, when they put us in
individual cells, although cells is scarcely the proper
word. The prison was the usual mud, stone and
wattle affair of most buildings in the North West
except barracks and bungalows.

I didn't fancy hanging very much and I knew that
although as a last resort I might fall back on dis-
closing my real identity, I should have some difficulty
in proving that now, and rather than go to the trouble
of investigating my supposed origins they might
well string me up along with the rest and no one
but the prison officials would be any the wiser.
It was distinctly depressing, and I had to think pretty
quickly to get myself out of that jam. There was
only one satisfactory way of getting out and that was
breaking the gaol—a difficult job in a spot surrounded
by soldiers and civilians.

I had to take my chance when the havildar on duty
came in to give me bread and water. He was pretty
tough that man, a tall fellow from the hills who knew

how to use his hands as well as his rifle. But it was him or myself and he didn't have the thought of a hanging the next morning to spur his efforts. I got him down quite quickly by using a rather unpleasant trick, and without going into details, I left him there without much chance of waking up again and crept out. It was just getting light and I had a strip of open ground to negotiate, posted with sentries, before I could make the road and cross into cover. I knew the alarm would not be raised for a few minutes, since the man who had brought me my food would naturally be expected to be absent for a time on duty.

I tore off my *kamis* (shirt), and rolled my loose trousers round my loins to make myself less conspicuous, then ran for it. I got about half-way when I was spotted. A report rang out and I felt a shot whine past my head. God, how I ran! I expected at any minute to hear the entire cantonment after me. But for some reason I never discovered the alarm could not have been raised for quite a while after that shot was fired. Whether in the dim light the sentry thought he had been mistaken and perhaps shot at some stray dog, or whether some sort of red tape process prevented an immediate turnout, I don't know. In any case I got clear away into the hills above Peshawar and at sunrise was making my way through the narrow ravine which cut across the border and along which Khaidar

Khan had so often made his mysterious descents upon the native city.

I intended to find the remaining members of the band and explain the two-faced betrayal of Kudar Bux who had sold the life of Khaidar Khan for six thousand rupees. At least then, by shewing myself, my name would not be a reproach among the Afridi fighting men, and it would not be one that the survivors would swear a feud against to be pursued relentlessly until honour was satisfied. I felt sorry for the collector of the blood-money, and sorrier still for his women folk and relations. I knew the oath. "Let them be torn out root and branch!"

When at last I reached the village of Khaidar Khan I was received with looks blacker than thunder. My greeting and explanations were heard in silence. It was obvious that I was not trusted, and I guessed they had been discussing me in my absence.

"What, then, is thy purpose," I asked at last, "now that the English, God's curse upon them, have slain Khaidar Khan, and a score of women are widows to-night?"

"We shall soon tire of sitting in the hills," one of them replied. "Go thy way, Yusuf Khan, and we will do likewise."

I could perceive that this was a polite suggestion to remove myself if I valued my life, and as for those men returning to their villages to become small farmers, I knew that was very unlikely before some attempt had been made to avenge the death of their fellow-raiders.

I heard some time later that the English were mistaken in supposing that by killing Khaidar Khan they would disperse the whole band. His son stepped into his shoes and proved even more troublesome than his father!

II

From then on for some months I became a lone wolf once more, living my own life in the only fashion which now appealed to me. I was not without resources as a result of the numerous raids in which I had participated with Khaidar Khan and I lived the life of the average Afridi who is not too scrupulous about how he earns a living and leaves husbandry to the dwellers in the plains.

After a while I began to make solitary night excursions into the cantonment at Peshawar, helping myself to what was useful in the European bungalows. Sometimes money, more often rifles and revolvers. They are valuable currency in themselves over the border as I have explained before. It wasn't very much more risky this way than it had been when I was running in the consignments from Bushire.

The method was simple. I would strip completely naked except for a loosely tied loin-cloth (loose, because it might be grabbed in an emergency and would come off), shave my beard and grease myself from head to foot in cheetah-fat. It may surprise the reader to learn that the beautiful hunting-leopard he has seen in the cat-house at the Zoo with the descriptive label: "Cheetah: partially domes-ticated and used for hunting in Northern India and Persia" has other uses, no less distinguished because the beast is dead. When the grease from the dead cheetah is boiled down it is frequently used by marauding tribesmen in the way I have mentioned since no dog, however fierce or dutiful, will come near the smell!

After that it requires only stealth and a certain knowledge of European habits to gain access to a bungalow at dead of night when I would take what I could find. There was a grimly humorous side to these excursions. Most of the residents employ a *chowkidar* as night watchman, and frequently one man has the duty of watching perhaps three bungalows. He walks round all night calling out at intervals: "*Chow-ki-dar!*" which is supposed to prove he is awake and doing his job. As a matter of fact it also lets the night raider know exactly where he is, which the poor devil is anxious for us to do! He knows he is best away when that sort of mouse is playing and a knife in the belly is painful.

If I was 'operating' in a room in which someone was sleeping and they happened to awake, a gleaming *peshkoza* at the throat and the word "*Chuprao!*" (Shut up!) would effectively silence all but the most obstinate cases. The very sight of the dread Afridi is enough for most civilians to be stricken dumb. On one occasion, however, I was very nearly caught.

I was in the bungalow of a certain officer some time after midnight. All was quiet and I got busy in the bedroom. The room was empty, and I supposed the owner was out at a dance or dining with brother officers. It seemed quite simple, especially as there in its case was an excellent heavy-bore sporting rifle and several boxes of ammunition. Quite suddenly a torch was turned on me and I swung round, to find myself confronted with a middle-aged man in pyjamas covering me with a heavy service revolver.

"Drop that gun!" he barked in Pashtu. I knew he meant business, and he was looking at me meaningly. "Son of a pig, I will take thee to the police!" He backed me into a chair and put the rifle which I had taken from its case safely out of reach. Then with a contempt which I could not help but admire he turned his back on me and started to dress himself. He was a powerfully built man and I daresay reckoned himself more than my match even without his revolver. A thing he might have been, if he had not forgotten one thing. In my loose cotton loin-cloth *I still carried my knife!* While his back was still turned to me I crept up and caught him a blow on the skull with the haft, which stretched him insensible before he had uttered a sound.

o

I stole out of that bungalow a few minutes later, with the sporting rifle and the officer's Webley-Scott service revolver. The native servants had slept through it all.

Another dodge well known across the border was procuring Lee-Enfields from beneath soldiers sleeping in the lines. I say beneath, since the practice of sleeping beside the rifle was abandoned on the frontier many years before. Scores were taken mysteriously from under the very noses of the sentries every night by the cunning raiders. So the rule was changed that each man should sleep on a trench specially dug to hold his rifle, over which was placed the ground-sheet and blanket, and on top of it all the owner of the rifle. It would seem impossible to reach the gun without disturbing the man. Nevertheless, in spite of this, rifles disappeared nightly in numbers, while the soldiers swore that nothing had disturbed them. Not only that, but the blankets began to disappear too. The method used, at any rate by the Afridi, was simple as it is efficacious.

First of all, let it be remembered that for the possession of such a valuable thing as a rifle, the thief is quite prepared to work all night, if necessary, and to filch one from beneath a sleeping man requires both time and patience. Having reached the objective, that is to say, passed the sentries and got inside the lines—a fairly simple matter for the cunning Afridi—a victim is selected, preferably, of course, one who is apparently a heavy sleeper. After a while, the sleeper's ear is tickled, very gently, with a feather. He may stir slightly in his sleep, but in ninety-nine cases out of a hundred he will not wake. This tickling is continued at intervals of, say, ten minutes, until as an almost invariable rule, the sleeper will turn over in his sleep and roll off the coveted rifle and blanket. After that, of course, the gun is as good as gone. Simple, isn't it? And yet as far as I know the British have never realised that that is what is done night after night, and accounts for the apparently miraculous disappearance of service rifles from impossible positions.

Even when sleeping in barracks, rifles were not safe until the introduction of an arms-rack, sunk in solid concrete, which could be bolted every night by means of an iron bar!

III

So life went on for months, full enough of excitement, although I did not look at it in that way, my life always in danger, as much from a clansman's bullet as a soldier's, or the hangman's rope.

But it was small meat after what I had been used to, and I began to think of chancing a return to Kabul to see how the market in small arms was progressing up there. I was running a grave risk of detection, of course, not only of re-arrest by the police after I had been supposedly banished into India, but there might well be persons in the city who suspected I was implicated in the death of Abdul Rahim. I do not wish to convey by this that I was a man 'wanted for murder' in the western sense, but if they knew his blood was upon my head, friends or relatives would take an early opportunity of avenging themselves. However, I had begun to feel dissatisfied with life in the hills and Kabul had certain attractions for me besides the prospect of re-entering the gun trade. . . .

At length I made up my mind to take the risk once more, and after buying myself some fresh clothes I took the caravan route to the city.

CHAPTER XV

A NIGHT FLIGHT

I

As I entered the city of Kabul once again, although I did not know it, I was on the threshold of my final adventure on the wrong side of the border. And for the second time in my life I was to have its whole course altered through a woman!

I had been in the city only a few days, being careful to avoid the bazaars where I might be recognised (although beyond hennaing my beard[1] I had not troubled to alter my appearance) when curiosity prompted me one night to revisit the scene of my last brief stay in Kabul when I had settled my little account with Abdul Rahim (May his soul rot in hell!). They say that some irresistible impulse always prompts the killer to revisit the scene of his crime, and although I reckoned ridding the world of him no crime, perhaps it was that which took me there that night. I had hardly reached the spot, when a woman, unveiled and evidently in a great

---

[1] Contrary to misinformed general supposition this is not a sign that the wearer has visited Mecca but merely a device employed by elderly men to give them a more youthful appearance!

state of agitation, rushed out of the very house in which the officer had spent his last night, shrieking: "*Hakim! Hakim!*[1] There is one here who dies!"

I ran forward to meet her, and eventually managed to interpret her hysterical cries as meaning that one of the girls in the house was in a high fever. What she said was that devils were devouring her for she spoke in a strange tongue. I told her that I had some small knowledge of healing and asked to be shewn the 'patient', since I imagined if it was merely a question of administering a sedative, I could cope with it quite effectually and at the same time perhaps save the woman hours of misery while some quack of a native *hakim* was found.

She led me into the house to an upper room where, lying on a low divan covered only with a strip of brightly coloured silk, was the victim of the devils. The face was unusually pale and sallow and as I drew near I recognised it in an instant as that of the dancing girl I had spoken to on the roof of Sherif Ali's house in Peshawar, and who had called herself Nur Jehan! Here indeed was the long arm of coincidence. She stared at me without recognition as I felt her forehead, moaning unintelligibly from time to time. Then suddenly I caught a familiar word or two. Not of Pushtu nor Hindustani—but *English!* She was singing to herself what was unmistakably "Humpty-Dumpty sat on a wall"!

[1] Doctor.

I suppose my amazement must have shewn on my face for the woman who had brought me in cried: "Thou seest she dies. Aiee! It is as Allah wills!"

I shook my head gravely: "The hour is not yet," I told her. It was a fairly obvious case of malaria, as far as I could see, and that meant one thing— quinine. I told her to send quickly into the bazaars to try and procure some (there was a European dispensary in Kabul, one of the improvements effected by the old Amir Abdur Rahman, which supplied a number of ordinary remedies to the bazaars). I impressed on her that the girl was on no account to be disturbed by the other women in the house who were already crowding and giggling at the entrance.

The woman (who was evidently the mistress of the house) assented and disappeared to despatch the errand. When she returned she told me that the girl was one of a troupe of dancers reserved exclusively for the Amir's durbars and occasional personal delectation, and she was afraid there might be trouble if the news of her death reached certain exalted quarters.

"Has she been here long?" I asked, wondering what had happened to the girl between that night on the roof-tops in Peshawar and now in this crooked street in Kabul.

"She is still young, O *hakim*. A virgin," replied the woman. It was evidently not her business to give information about her charges and I realised I should have to wait until I could talk to Nur Jehan herself.

She was still restless and from time to time repeating snatches of nursery-rhyme in unmistakable English. At length the quinine arrived and I dosed her, leaving instructions for her treatment and suggesting that I should revisit the house the next day.

I was received with considerable respect when I reached the house again and was informed gravely that the devils had left the girl in the night and that she now spoke with her own tongue. Even so, she did not recognise me immediately, although I suppose that was hardly surprising, but when I called her by name and mentioned Peshawar city she seemed pleased to think that I remembered her. She was quite lucid now, and talked vulubly in Pushtu. Suddenly I sprang a question to her in English, but her look of blank astonishment seemed too genuine to be simulated.

"In what tongue dost thou speak, Yusuf Khan?" she asked.

"The tongue of *rishtiyeh*,[1] Nur Jehan," I replied guardedly, "spoken by the sons of the father of lies, the English."

"Why dost thou speak thus to me?"

"When the sickness was upon thee, it was in that tongue that thou thyself spoke."

[1] Lies.

The girl laughed, evidently supposing that I was joking. However, my curiosity was thoroughly aroused and I told her to pretend to be ill for some time in order that I might come and see her and talk to her. As long as I performed my services as *hakim* I commanded a certain respect among the other women of the house which made my visits quite simple.

On the third occasion I saw her, Nur Jehan volunteered some information about herself and how she had reached Kabul. She told me she had been living for as long as she could remember with her mother in Peshawar city and had been trained as a dancing girl. Her youth and good looks had provided them both with quite a decent living and she looked forward without any regret to the fate which nearly always befalls such girls when mere dancing cannot earn them enough. Like thousands of her sisters she would enter the oldest profession in the world. . . .

It seemed that one night, one of the periodic raids on Peshawar by a party of border tribesmen had been centred in a district in which she was dancing and she had been carried off into the hills with the rest of the spoils. After a rather unpleasant week among the uncouth raiders she had suddenly been taken to Kabul and there entered the house she was now in. I imagine she had been sold for a very decent price.

As she described it there seemed to be nothing particularly unusual in all this. It was the will of Allah and had happened many times before to women of the border cities. Some court official visiting the house had drawn the attention of the Amir himself to her and she had become a member of the company of dancing girls reserved for him until such time as he grew tired of them or she lost her looks. She told me that she was happy enough but missed her mother and the familiar surroundings of Peshawar. Of course, she had long given up any hope of return, and in the manner of Eastern women was quite resigned to her fate. As a dancing girl, she went unveiled and would never marry. It was as Allah had willed, praised be his name!

I told her as much as I thought was necessary of my own adventures since I had seen her and that I too wished to return to Peshawar. I naturally did not want to reveal the real purpose of my presence in Kabul and told her that I was afraid to go down into the border country since I thought that Khaidar Khan's son had sworn a blood-feud against me. As a matter of fact, since my encounter with Nur Jehan, my ideas about once more engaging myself in the traffic in arms had begun to recede, and I wondered if perhaps I had not had enough of all that and be better advised to go down country again and re-establish my relations with the firm of Mukerjee.

At any rate, I certainly had no intention of returning to a European mode of living. I suppose what was really at the back of my mind, although I did not care to confess it to myself at that moment, was to reach the comparative safety of British India with the girl Nur Jehan. I may have had some vague ideas of a sort of attachment with her. I have forgotten my feelings, but at all events I suggested to her privately that she might accompany me.

Now the chances of getting a girl in her position even out of the city, far less out of Afghanistan, are about as great as if I was contemplating robbing the Amir's zenana itself.

She was regarded, for the time being at any rate, as part of the Amir's personal property and her disappearance would soon raise hue and cry with the direst penalty for anyone responsible. As I had already had a sample of Afghan punitive methods, I frequently wonder what on earth possessed me to be so crazy as to make the attempt.

However, I did, and it had a most unfortunate conclusion. At first Nur Jehan would not hear of accompanying me. Much as she longed to return to Peshawar and her old associations she was much too frightened of the consequences should our flight miscarry.

I told her that she must take her opportunity now, since while she was still sick her disappearance would be less likely to be noticed for a few hours. I told her I would arrange to procure two ponies which would carry us beyond the city limits fairly quickly and that with my knowledge of the hill country we could probably evade detection until we reached the neighbourhood of Ali Musjid. Then we could wait until the next caravan came down and go down through the Khyber with it.

Everything worked well enough up to a point. Soon after midnight on the day we had arranged, I left two ponies tethered in an alley not far from the house. I had procured a long white *burka* for the girl to wear, which as it covers the wearer from head to foot, only leaving a tiny space for the eyes, would at once serve as an effective concealment and avert suspicion. Unveiled women on horseback are a rarity in the East!

I waited for a time, crouched in the shadows, listening to the strains of music and laughter which emanated from the more active part of the establishment, wondering if perhaps the girl's nerve had failed at the last moment and the flight never be made. Suddenly she appeared at my side, having evidently made her exit from some different direction. As I caught her hand and hurried her along towards the ponies she laughed softly and said: "It is well that doors open both ways, Yusuf Khan."

The narrow crooked streets were deserted at this hour, save for an occasional pariah dog, and

after she had put the *burka* over her head we mounted
the horses unobserved and rode out of Kabul, as I
hoped, for the last time. I figured we had at the
most an hour before some sort of alarm would be
raised and quite possibly we should be pursued.
There was a good chance, on the other hand, that
the city would be searched first in which case we
could be well into the hills before it occurred to
anyone that we might have left Kabul. In any
event, I was hoping that her disappearance
would not immediately be connected with myself
(as there was no apparent reason why it should)
and as luck would have it I was right in all my
guesses.

Long before dawn we were many miles from
Kabul among the narrow passes and limestone crags
of the Suliman mountains. Just before sunrise
we halted for the first time. It was both useless
and dangerous to travel further before dusk, on
account of the intense heat and the possibility of
attack by some marksman hidden in the rocks. I
chose a spot which afforded excellent shelter and
concealment for us, and a little trickle of a stream
running down into the plain below gave water
for the ponies. Being on the northern side of a hill, a
few patches of turf and scrub here and there gave
them a little fodder while we lay in the cool shade of a
shallow cave. I made a few cakes from the contents
of my saddle bag and cooked them on a little fire of

twigs and brush. Nur Jehan was tired from the long
ride, apart from the fact that she was really in no
condition (after her fever) to undertake the hundred
and sixty mile journey from Kabul to the frontier
post of Jamrud. I began to be sorry that I had not
given consideration of this sort a little more weight
in making my hasty decision. The girl slept all
day and seemed still tired when I woke her at dusk
to prepare to push on. I hoped with luck to make
fifty or sixty miles before dawn again but as we
were as far as possible avoiding the caravan route
I was not sure just how much longer I was making
the journey. The narrow paths along the cliffs were
slow going for the ponies and after a time I decided
for the sake of saving time to take to the accepted
road for a few miles. I might have known better,
I suppose, especially as the moon was bright enough
to make it almost daylight.

We skirted several villages, with their towers
silhouetted against the dim background of the hills,
and I wondered how many unseen eyes watched
us from within. Two travellers, one a woman!
My own Afridi life told me this would seem like
easy money to any hillman with a good rifle.

However, luck remained with us and once more
at sunrise we lay up among the rocks, sleeping and
waiting for nightfall. I reckoned that the next
night's journey should see us within a reasonable
distance of our objective, Ali Musjid. As it happened

it took us even further than that, but not at all in the way I anticipated!

II

We had gone, I suppose, about ten miles, keeping off the caravan route, winding in and out among the deep ravines, along narrow goat-tracks on which a stumble might mean a swift descent of a few hundred feet, when the girl began to complain that she was afraid to go further by this method and begged me to guide the horses down to where the going was less hard. I told her the route was watched by marauding tribesmen, just as I had often watched it myself, waiting for the opportunity to spend a swift bullet and gain the contents of a lonely traveller's purse. But she insisted that she would rather die that way than endure the agony of riding further like this, and since she certainly looked in pretty bad shape, and I was half afraid that in her weak condition she might well have a recurrence of the fever, I consented reluctantly and returned to the road down which the caravans wind slowly into British India.

The moon was still bright, and as it was fairly cold I urged the ponies into a canter, hoping at least to compensate for the risk we were taking by making better time.

The false dawn had just broken over the hills some hours later when I suddenly felt a sharp pain

in my shoulder and heard simultaneously the *ping*
of a rifle report! The pony reared and almost threw
me.

I yelled to the girl to beat her pony, although
for all I knew we might be riding towards the unseen
sharpshooter. The pain in my shoulder intensified
and I could feel the arm going numb. The girl
began to whimper, and I cursed her savagely,
catching her horse a blow on the flanks with my free
hand. At any moment I knew another shot would
follow, perhaps the last for one of us. A couple
of seconds later I heard the report and saw Nur
Jehan's beast stagger and throw her.

There was nothing for it but to dismount and
lift her up. If there was any chance of escape now
I had to take it quickly. I could see my shoulder
was bleeding pretty freely and I prayed against
the unconsciousness which I knew loss of blood
would bring. The girl had already fainted, or else
was dead, but somehow I dragged her on to the
pony and started off again. Only the poor light
could have saved our lives that night. A third
shot sang unpleasantly near my head and I heard
the report echo round the hills. The limp body
hanging across the saddle in front of me formed
some sort of support or I might well have fallen
off myself from sheer weakness. The scared animal
was bolting now, digging its hoofs hard into the
soft, dusty track and breathing hard. How far

we went like that I do not know. I remember
falling heavily and dragging the girl with me, after
which I suppose I fainted. It was broad daylight
when I came to and the pain in my shoulder
throbbed excruciatingly. We were lying in the
shadow of a tall group of boulders, the girl beside
me still.

A tall Pathan farmer with a rifle slung over his
shoulder was bending over me, and at first I thought
it must be the marksman of our unpleasant experience.
I felt utterly done, all my vitality sapped with loss
of blood, and remembering vaguely that we must
be near the frontier I asked him weakly to send down
to the nearest frontier post with a message that a sahib
was dying.

As no one could have looked less like a sahib
at that moment than I did he must have thought I
was mad, I suppose. But perhaps for that reason,
or something else I may have said, he evidently did
what I told him, for later I was roused again from
unconsciousness by a native havildar and three men
wearing the khaki of the Khyber Rifles.

We were taken down to the frontier post at Jamrud,
where I was placed technically under arrest pending
investigation. As a matter of fact I was treated
very decently by the English officer in charge, as
I suppose he was not very concerned about cross-
examining a sick man. He probably had a fair
idea of the sort of questioning I should get back

P

in Peshawar. I told him about the girl and he assured me that she would in all probability be sent direct to the native hospital in Peshawar.

The next day I was sent down to Peshawar General Hospital myself where my wound was dressed and I was put to bed until I was well enough to be questioned.

I realised, of course, that the game was up now and that I had 'blown the gaff' on myself. Yusuf Khan was, for the time being, at any rate, dead, and Douglas McHardie must come to life again and take the consequences.

When at length I was brought before the military authorities I was not surprised to find they took a pretty serious view of the whole thing. My carefully concocted explanations were laughed at and in fairness to the British Intelligence in India I must state here that they seemed to know a great deal indeed about my activities in the last few years, and had apparently been on the look-out for me for some time. The interrogation was more than thorough and I was kept up there for three weeks while wires buzzed between Simla and Peshawar. I must have seen about a dozen different officers, all with a different set of questions.

Although I was never able to confirm it, I still have a strong suspicion that it was the work of a British agent which landed me on the roadside outside Kabul as a suspected spy!

The net result of it all was the issue of a deportation order, and I was sent down to Bombay under military escort.

And Nur Jehan? I never saw her again, but while I lay in hospital I managed to get the doctor to find out what had happened to her. It appeared that the authorities had, on my reports and suspicions, discovered that her 'mother' was really her old ayah, whom they forced to confess, employed by her English parents, a colonel and his wife! While she was still a child they had both been killed in a frontier scrap and the ayah had escaped with the child and brought it up as her own. The woman had dyed the child's skin with some sort of absolutely impermeable colouring known to Pathan native doctors, of which I had heard before. European women have been taken across the border more often than has been allowed to come to light, and in such circumstances the process has its uses. But her name I never discovered, and what happened to her I don't know. Maybe one day I shall see her again. . . .

CHAPTER XVI

1914

I

As you may imagine I wasn't feeling too good about returning to the States in the role of deportee, apart from the fact that I had been away so long that I was certain I should now feel as strange as though I was in a foreign country.

I understood I was to be jailed again on reaching Bombay until the necessary formalities had been completed for my deportation and the next boat left, and spent most of the time in the train journey south gaining the confidence of my escort of two Tommies. When they had made up their minds that I was not going to give them any trouble, they proved very decent fellows and seemed quite interested in what I had to tell them of doings over the border. I made it fairly plain to them that I was pretty pleased to be shot of the whole darned thing with a free passage home into the bargain, with the result that they must have been highly surprised when on Bombay station they found their tame bird had flown. They were so sure of me that I was allowed to obey a call of nature unescorted and I skipped!

I managed to get into the crowded bazaar and out of my European clothes, as I knew that there I should be comparatively safe. Moreover, it was extremely necessary that I should remain lost since I fully realised that if I was arrested again it would mean a prison stretch in addition to eventual deportation. I tried several times to get word through to Mukerjee—I did not dare go near his office or house myself as I reckoned it would be watched—and at last I succeeded. He sent me a little money and a warning to lie low for some time while he would see what he could do for me.

Then, with a suddenness which seemed to me to be almost divine intervention on my behalf, came news of the declaration of war on August 4th, 1914!

Before a week had elapsed I decided to take a chance in the general excitement and offer myself as a volunteer. There was a wild rush in those early days among the British civilian population to get into the army and over to France. I guessed, and rightly as it proved, that I stood a fair chance of getting away with the general rush without too many questions asked.

By August 20th I had been drafted into the Royal Garrison Artillery and after ten days' training was sent down to Karachi to join the Expeditionary Force leaving for Europe.

II

Since war experiences have become a glut on the
literary market of the world I am not sufficiently
rash to imagine that mine would be of any special
interest to the reader.

I suppose my life was neither more nor less
pleasant than that of millions of others. After
being sent to France soon after my enlistment I was
made sergeant after three months, was wounded
on April 15th, 1915, and sent to No. 14 General
Hospital in Boulogne. In December, 1915, the
powers in Whitehall suddenly decided that Flanders'
mud was rather unsuitable for Indian troops and
the word went round that we were to be sent home.
There was considerable joy among the native regi-
ments at the prospect of returning to the tropical
sun. We went. Marseilles—Malta—Alexandria—
Port Said—Suez—*but not Karachi!* Almost within
sight of home we swung round north and west again
into the Persian Gulf and disembarked at Basra.

That was near enough for a lot of the Indian
units. Regarding the change of direction as a promise
broken by the British Government, hundreds of
them deserted and made their way overland across
the very country that I had traversed some years
before, back to India. Incidentally the mud at Basra
was even worse than in France. The day I arrived
we lost three wagons completely, submerged in the

ooze. In the stern-wheeler—H.i. I went up to
Sheikh Saad in Mesopotamia in which country I
remained for the duration, as we used to say. Perhaps
I was able to enjoy the war out there a little more
than most since I was thoroughly at home in that
type of country and the only thing which irked
me was army discipline. I was used enough to
fighting in all conscience, and death had come to
mean little enough after my experiences in Afghanistan; but organised, carefully drilled killing went
against the grain with me more than once, and I say
without regret that I was A.W.O.L. on several
occasions as a result of it.

Perhaps it will help you to understand my point
of view when I quote a single instance of this discipline I found so hard. I, a Moslem, was ordered by
my superior officer to strip and flog on a heap of
grain bags a non-combatant Arab, also a Moslem,
for some petty misdemeanour. My whole spirit
rebelled against this and I am bitterly ashamed of
it to this day.

When the Armistice found me at Mosul I was
asked if I was prepared to serve a further period
of two years. But I had had enough of military
discipline and, of course, refused. There was nothing in the world I wanted more than to be on my
own again.

I got my discharge some weeks later at Delhi,
and began to wonder what I was going to do.

CHAPTER XVII

GOOD-BYE TO INDIA

I

FROM Delhi I took the train down to Bombay again with the idea of once more seeking the assistance of my old friend Edeljibhoy Mukerjee. I had no thought of living elsewhere than in India where I had already spent so many of the best years of my life. There was small risk now, I considered, of being caught up again with the military authorities provided I steered clear of any trouble up in the north.

The old Parsee received me as ever most hospitably, and keeping the promise he had made me years before the war immediately gave me a job on a buying expedition. On his own recommendation I went this time to the south, to Bangalore. For my own safety as well as peace of mind I can assure the reader that at this time I was more than anxious to settle down as a respectable citizen and lead the orderly life of a law-abiding business man. I could make quite a comfortable living working with Mukerjee and I knew my job. There seemed to be no reason, therefore, why I should not be able to pursue my purpose. But once again Fate, or Allah, had decreed otherwise.

I had arranged to take over a bungalow for occupation in Bangalore from a pleasant English couple by the name of Parker, who were returning home, and they suggested that for the few days before they moved out I might care to go and stay with them.

Now Mrs. Parker was one of those ladies who rather fancy that they are possessed of a psychic streak, second sight or whatever it's called, and a day or two after my arrival she selected me as a likely victim to try her skill. We were sitting one night after dinner talking when she managed to steer the conversation round to that particular subject and suggested she should give me a demonstration of her supposed gifts. In the usual way she asked me for something I always carried about with me and I gave her a coin I had picked up at the beginning of the war and had in my pocket ever since. She clutched it and closed her eyes for a bit and then said suddenly: "Well, really this is extraordinary. I have a distinct feeling that you won't be living in this bungalow after all, or even in Bangalore."

Parker and I laughed, as only that day I had completed arrangements for a fairly lengthy stay.

"Anything else?" I prompted.

"Yes," she said. "I feel you are going further

north. Not Bombay, north of that. Up in the mountains where there is snow but not many trees."

She told me a lot more nonsense, all of which I forgot until, at the end of the week I heard that there was still trouble up in Waziristan!

All my good resolutions vanished. I felt I would give my soul to get back into the hill country, and enlistment in a mountain battery proved easy enough. I wrote a hasty apology to my firm and within ten days I was in Dera Ismail Khan, the base of the Waziristan operations.

From there without much loss of time we were sent up to Jandola and thence to Tank where things were happening. The country up there is even worse than that to the north of Peshawar. Almost devoid of vegetation, a mass of hills and waterless ravines, it is some of the most difficult fighting country in the world, I suppose, which is why the Wazirs and Mahsud tribes who were causing the trouble have so often managed to hold the British frontier forces engaged so often and so long.

To my disappointment I didn't see a great deal of actual fighting, as soon after my arrival I was detached from the battery and put on to dealing with the supplies. Here, however, I soon found that opportunity of a different kind awaited me, and I became a part of the great *tikki*[1] racket which

[1] Contract.

has its ramifications wherever the Indian army is, and which is why so many men return to England after service in India with pockets filled with more than their normal pay.

I was detailed to make arrangements in villages surrounding the fighting area with various *tikkidars*[1] for the supply of food for men and animals utilizing the resources of the country to supplement that sent up by the convoys from the supply basis, and I soon found myself in a position to make a very handsome profit on almost every 'buy'.

Since there was no form of check-up other than documentary, the game was played simply enough. It is worked in this manner:

I would obtain a chit for, say, Rs. 5,000 from the officer in charge, to buy grain or *bhusa* for the mules, and go to a *tikkidar* who would give me a receipt for the full amount, but supply only Rs. 2,000 worth. This would be duly delivered, and the receipt handed in and sent down to the record office. In due course I should be handed a 'mysterious' packet containing Rs. 1,500, my share of the profits on the deal with the government!

The extent of this racket is simply amazing and the odd part about it is that everyone is 'in the know'—even the officers—and yet the practice continues unabated. I heard while I was up there of two sergeants who had cleared Rs. 30,000 in a year!

[1] Indian merchants licensed by the Government to supply the troops.

But they evidently overdid it because they were exposed and given six months in Poona gaol and dismissed the army. Nevertheless, when they were released they opened a large garage and repair works in Simla under the very nose of the people who had sentenced them, and I believe are still there doing very well!

Another means of augmenting my income at that time was presented by fluctuations in the exchange. A soldier was allowed to send his money away through the Field Post Office at the rate of Rs. 7½ to the £. He was paid at the rate of Rs. 13 —a net gain of Rs. 5½ to every £. I not only drew every cent of pay I could get but I arranged a constant flow of money coming through to me from old Mukerjee. My only regret was that the Post Office would only accept Rs. 400 in one day.

This went on for ten months when, the Mahsuds subdued for the moment, I got my discharge and decided to say good-bye for ever this time to the army and all its works. I took the train down to Bombay again with the idea of taking a short holiday and sorting things out. I was feeling thoroughly unsettled in myself by now, uncertain whether to resume relations again with Mukerjee or strike out alone in some as yet undecided direction. My mind was made up for me on this point, however, by the discovery on arrival in Bombay that the

Rs. 7½—Rs. 7-8 annas.

old man was dead. His sons, who were carrying on the business, I did not know very well, and although they assured me they would like me to continue to work for them, I did not feel inclined to take the job on.

The net result was that I spent almost a year in Bombay doing very little but wonder what I should do next and spending most of my money.

II

Then one day I made up my mind, quite suddenly, to go to England. I had only been there once, on leave from France for a few days, and it may have been the effect of hearing so many people talk longingly of 'home' that made me decide to visit it myself. I had no idea of what I should do when I got there but as so often before I left that to chance or Fate. In any case, the beginning of 1922 saw me in London with the remainder of my money invested in a garage.

But a year of that was more than enough for me and I found that life in a huge city went badly against the grain. Within twelve months although I was doing reasonably well, I sold out to a man who, incidentally, still owes me half the money!

I do not wish the reader to suppose that I just threw up my business without any idea of what I was going to do. There was a certain method in my madness. Among the customers of my garage in South London was a man with whom I became rather friendly, largely on the grounds that I was a Californian. He himself was an Englishman (I don't think he had ever been to America) but he was managing director of a company which controlled various concerns in all parts of the world, a gold mine in Australia, a ranch in Argentina and among other things a sizeable orange-grove in my native state.

As we grew more friendly I learnt from him that he was not at all satisfied with the results shewn from the orange groves during the past two years. It was situated just outside San Bernardino, about sixty miles from Los Angeles, and for quite a time after the company had purchased it, it continued to shew a very good profit. Now, however, the crops had fallen away badly and he was not satisfied that the place was being run properly by the manager.

I happened to mention one day that I was getting fed up with London, and that England itself was too small to hold me, and that I thought of either returning to India or going back to the States if I could only think of what to do. He asked me suddenly if I would entertain a proposition connected with his business out there. I told him that as I hadn't been in the country for nearly twenty years I should be just as strange out there as he would. However, I asked what his ideas were, and he suggested I might like to take a job as a sort of assistant

supervisor and report confidentially to him on what
was happening on the orange-grove. As he offered
my expenses out there and a fair salary, you can
imagine I jumped at it. The opportunity was too
good to pass up, and I must confess to a certain
hankering to see California once more and get the
chance of seeing some of the places I had experienced in my adventurous youth. I couldn't help
smiling to myself at the contrast between the way
I left the States and my return.

I crossed to New York first class in the White
Star Liner *Cedric*. I bet my old man would have
turned in his grave to see me after the dismal future
he had foretold for me!

CHAPTER XVIII

CALIFORNIA REVISITED

I

I WENT straight through from New York to the ranch, where I was expected and was made as reasonably welcome as my rather unreasonable appearance deserved, by the manager. Of course, I didn't know the first thing about orange growing and I had spent most of the time on the journey out "mugging it up". I saw no point in pretending that I was an expert and I think it was that fact that enabled me to become more acceptable to the staff already out there. Most of them were pretty regular guys and I didn't fancy my job as informer very much. You will have guessed by now that my scruples are few, but telling tales is one of the things I don't care about doing. Although I was on the grove for a year it wasn't long before I discovered just what was wrong.

The State of California requires a percentage of the profits of every orange-growing concern to be set aside and put back into the land, which after all is only common sense in any sort of farming.

It appeared that in this particular grove, nothing had been put into the soil for about three years, and the whole place was farmed out and the land used up. The assignment for fertilisation appeared as usual in the books but I rather fancy that the manager and the 'hands' had appropriated it and made a handsome cut. When my suspicions grew to certainty I notified the directors in London and began to wonder whether my usefulness had finished.

I got a letter from my London friend, thanking me for the explanation of their loss of profits and asking me if I would like to take over full control when they had sacked the manager. In spite of the financial inducement I had to write back and decline his offer since I figured it wouldn't take a great deal of sense for anyone else to guess how I got that job, and I should probably have a job to get anyone to work for me. Apart from that, it would seem to me like dirty work and I didn't want to take it.

In the end I cleared out after being there just under a year and headed back to 'Frisco. I couldn't bear to pass up the chance of finding my old associates now that I was so near after all this time, and anyway I wanted news of Inez and my kid.

I arrived in 'Frisco early one morning, and the first thing I did when I stepped off the train was

to walk straight down Market Street to Kearney
and hunt up "The Thousand Delights". As I
mentioned some way back, all I found was a soda
pop mill and I had the unusual experience of sitting in my own bar (now all plate glass and basket
chairs) and ordering up a hamburger and coffee
from a cute little blondie who'd have lasted just
five minutes there in the old days, except that she
wasn't even thought of at that time.

I couldn't get any information there of course—
nobody even knew my name—so I went to the Public
Library and after half an hour with the directory I
dug up a couple of old acquaintances. I learned
from them that Inez had sold out on me about a
month after I disappeared and skipped after the
boy died. Nobody had heard of her for many years.

I went up and had a look at the kid's grave,
thinking that perhaps after all it was just as well.
I hadn't done a thing for him and even now I don't
suppose I could.

II

I didn't feel so good about staying in 'Frisco
after that. I went back to Los Angeles, and out
to Riverside in the orange country where I met an
Englishman named Cotton, who was a grower. He
told me flat there was nothing in it and he was
going to get out, but I had different ideas about a
well-run grove after what I had learned up at San
Bernardino and he got the shock of his life when

I offered him a price on his holdings, subject to inspection. We went out the next day (he was farming in the same area as I had worked, out near El Casco), and made a deal that day.

The time had come, I told myself once again, to settle down and become once and for all a peaceful citizen. I persuaded myself I had seen and done enough for one lifetime and a comfortable living in pleasant surroundings was what I really wanted. How I worked on that orange grove! For six months I sweated and toiled, improving, spending every penny I could get, incorporating the latest improvements and finally getting to hate the very sight of an orange tree! Once again I felt I would willingly lose all to get on the road again, to clear right out of it and feel I was free. I sold out at a dirt price and went back to the place which had been in my mind so often as I slaved away in the sweltering Californian sun—*up into the Yukon!*

CHAPTER XIX

BACK TO 40 BELOW

I

I WAS thrilled as a kid at the thought of going North again and getting back into 'man's country' and even the passage to Skagway with a mob of schoolmarms and guide book readers didn't damp my enthusiasm. I went over the Chilcoot to White Horse in a railway coach this time and took a stern-wheeler river boat down to Dawson. All the way in I had my memories, my ghosts with me, Hansen and Forbes and the rest. Some of them, I knew, would still be up there.

As I trod the sidewalks of Dawson, now unfamiliar and hardly recognisable, my ghosts walked with me. It was the queerest feeling I ever had. I found the old saloon where I 'swamped' for my first pay-dirt. They were just pulling it down, and the demolition gang had panned nearly a hundred dollars of dust from under the floor boards. I felt like telling them it belonged to me!

In the whole of Dawson City I only found one man I knew—Jack Doyle, the ex-sergeant of

"Mounties" who was running the "Principal" Hotel. There was quite a mob up there who had heard of me, it seemed, and when Doyle sent the word around that I was 'in', I could have swum in booze. I never reckoned I should turn up in Dawson in the role of old sourdough and spin yarns of how we used to manage in the earlies! But I felt good to think my name was still remembered.

I had made up my mind to go out to the creeks again (there's still plenty of gold in the Yukon) and as it was the end of summer I bought an outfit and winter's grub—incidentally cans of stuff we never dreamed of once—and started out. The first place I came to, about twenty miles up the creeks, was Shute and Wells' old saloon, deserted, broken-down and ramshackle now, but still peopled with memories for me, the dancing, the faro tables, the women and the liquor! There was a rusty old iron stove there which gave me the idea of passing the night in the place, but too many old faces came and sat around with me—the first case of nerves I ever knew. I couldn't stick it and after a couple of hours I rolled my blanket and cleared out again before I went mad.

The next day I managed to locate three of my old claims, only to find them now just "tailings"— rock and stones thrown out at the back of a machine-driven dredger. About a mile down the creek I saw the dredger itself, just finishing for the winter. I had been told in Dawson that great corporations like the Guggenheim's had bought practically all the old claims in the Yukon and were dredging them out by machine and making money fast. It's a very different story from my experiences with a bucket and a hand-windlass thirty foot below the ice.

Eventually I leased five hundred yards of bench from the operating company. ('Benches' is the name given to the sides of creeks being worked by the dredging companies, but which are outside the area they estimate to take into the dredger track. These benches can be leased for 15% of their yield—if any.) I worked it the whole of that winter and when the spring came and brought the water with it, I washed my dirt, only to discover that my net earnings after paying the company and settling for my outfit and stores was barely a hundred dollars.

That was precious little use to me, and I decided to try fresh fields and pastures new. Accordingly I mushed out to the Stewart River country which lies about one hundred and forty miles or so above Dawson. I was not after gold this time, either, but galena, silver-bearing lead ore, in which it was reported that quite a few prospectors were making good money.

I located it soon after I got there and after I had recorded I was so darned sure I could see a million that I bought an option on every claim I could lay my hands on. I managed this pretty cheaply, too, because the rest of the bunch in that section didn't seem to think much of it. However, I was pretty excited about the assayer's report, and I begged and borrowed every penny I could get and went back to San Francisco. I had an idea.

On my last visit I had met a lawyer during the course of my investigations about my 'wife' and I put up to him the suggestion of forming a company to exploit these claims properly and buy more options.

He fell for it immediately, and so, unfortunately did a lot of other people. I went back a few months later as a director, with a heap of machinery and every prospect of getting rich quick.

Within a year I was out again, flat broke, and ten thousand dollars in debt! Worse still, while I was working the barren claims we got the news that one of the spots where I had previously located and turned down had become another bonanza—and that was Keno Hill, Mayo, one solid mass of argentiferous galena!

If I had known a little more about it I don't suppose I should have been so crazy as to start floating companies since the cost of bringing machinery up there is colossal. It is only worth while to pay freight on the very finest grade ore, and labour is almost impossible to obtain owing to the certainty of arsenical lead poisoning for any man working after his first two months.

Then again, the Stewart river is only open water for about six weeks in the year, and with all these circumstances militating against you, it's got to be a pretty rich find to become a paying proposition.

II

After that little episode I wasn't very keen on going back to 'Frisco where I knew the shareholders would be looking for me, so with the few hundred dollars I had pulled out of the mess for myself I went down to Vancouver, B.C., once more out and with precious little prospect. I hung around there until most of my money was gone, spent the last fifty dollars on a glorious jag and woke up one morning with a fat head and the idea of going east to New York! And once again I had the old problem to face. The idea was good enough, but the difficulty was how?

CHAPTER XX

ON THE RUN AGAIN!

I

GETTING across the continent of America on nothing is not particularly simple, far less simple than before the war in any case, and there was nothing for it but to get a job and try to save the money.

A firm of contractors in Vancouver was recruiting men at that time for a tunnelling job in the Rockies and I offered myself, with a number of assumed qualifications, for the job of construction boss. I got the job and a twenty dollar 'transportation' advance which I'm afraid altered my mind about blasting through the mountain side, for I got off the train and hopped a freighter as far as Calgary. I had an object in going there since a fellow I had met in France during the war had given me his address in case I should ever get out that way. I remembered his name and the street and I thought I would chance finding him to see what was doing to help me get further east.

I found his widow—my pal had got his after I left for the East—and when I made myself known

she seemed pretty pleased to see me. Without
going into details I found also that she was looking
for another husband as well, and since I preferred
nursing cows to nursing kids, I went down to Patsy
Burn's stockyards in Calgary and collected the job
of escorting a couple of car loads of live stock down
to Montreal. I lit out without even saying good-
bye to the widow. I guess I'd had enough bad
luck with women before!

On the way down a bum hopped on the cattle-
freighter and I kept him in with the steers for a
couple of days. It was someone to talk to and I
got a fair amount of useful information on the hobo
situation at the time which I felt might come in
handy before I made my objective. We used to
spend a good deal of time shooting crap, and as
he didn't have any money to make the game a bit
exciting I played him for his gun. He was carrying
a fully loaded six-chambered revolver he'd lifted
from somewhere (naturally I asked no questions!)
and by the time we got to Montreal the gun was
mine. I was pretty pleased when he handed it over.

I delivered the steers and began to wonder what
Montreal was like when you're flat broke, and
wanting to get to New York. I didn't stay really
long enough to find out because the day after I
arrived I was fool enough to have the idea I could
short-circuit my financial difficulties with the aid
of that gun!

I stuck a guy up as he was going home that night. It was pretty late and quiet, too, and he looked the kind who'd be too scared to make any fuss when he saw I meant business. But I was mistaken. He squealed like a stuck pig and I had to hit him hard before I got his wad, because he had seen my face and wasn't likely to forget it. He had a decent sized roll, too, but I cursed him the moment he went down with his face all bloody. The stench of blood was on my hands again, just when I had almost forgotten it! I had to get going, and get going fast after that.

I got down without encountering any further trouble to Huntingdon, about five miles from the United States border, and there, of course, I was stuck—on the run with no papers. I hung around for as long as I dared and started walking down the bank of the Chateauguay River which has its source in the States. At one time I thought I might swim across, but concluded that was too risky. I was beginning to get worried about my chances of ever reaching New York City when I happened across an old man with a shack on the river bank who told me he was a fisherman. He talked just enough to give me an idea when he said he had a permit to fish *both* sides of the river, because he had a boat and would in any case attract no attention, and I had money.

Inside an hour I'd talked him into it. It was

expensive but necessary and I landed on the United States bank about 4 a.m. the following morning. From the way he knew how to ask for money, I guess that old fisherman had been used in the booze-running game before ever I met him, since a lot of the stuff was coming through about there to Malone in New York State about that time.

I went down to Malone that day, bought myself some food and made my way across the Adirondacks. I took occasional odd jobs, and bummed rides for the next two hundred miles until I landed up one night in Albany where I managed to work a passage as pearl diver (washer up) in one of the Hudson River pleasure boats going between there and New York.

So here I was in the Big City at last, but arrived as so often before with nothing but the clothes I stood up in—and the gun. That went straight to the pawnshop to buy me a meal and lodging for a night or two and give me a chance to look around. Beyond passing through on my way to San Bdo. I had never set foot in New York before but I wasn't worried much about prospects from all I had heard.

II

I got a tip on the boat to get down on the lower East Side where things were cheap and about my third day in the city found me in the Bowery (not quite as cleaned up as the cops would have you suppose).

They say if you hang around New York long enough you'll meet every one you ever knew but I certainly gave a howl of delight when I recognised a guy on the opposite side walk as Butch Callahan.

Butch had been one of the best of my boys in "The Thousand Delights" back in the old days in 'Frisco and just about as tough a young pug then as anyone cared to find out. He had left the place before my own sudden departure and I had been of some service to him at the time managing to get him off a homicide charge. He got in a tangle in my saloon one night with a bird who thought he'd been gypped, and who was mug enough to die a few days later after Butch Callahan's treatment!

We pumped each other's hands for about ten minutes before we got down to talking, and when I suggested he might know somewheres we could get a drink and yarn for a bit, I had another shock when he told me in all earnestness that he'd given up all that sort of thing and would I come to his *prayer-meeting* that night!

I didn't know what to make of it, but I went along and I'm afraid was nearly paralysed with laughter to see Butch's well-scarred homely mug, complete with pug's trademark of a cauliflower ear, standing up there yelling about hell-fire and brotherly love one minute, and belting the hell the next out of some bum who had come in for a row or a sleep and was doing either of them too loud!

He told me when it was over how he had come to New York several years before and at first had got mixed up with the boys on the East side, found the going too rotten for him and suddenly got religion. He was perfectly serious about it, too, although I had a job to keep a straight face.

When I had seen him once or twice he told me he'd be glad for me to help around the mission hall for a while until I got fixed somewhere, cleaning up and attending to the disorderly element where necessary. It wasn't quite my idea of success in the Big City but it gave me the chance to look about and keep my head above water.

At the same time it was helping the boys to keep theirs out of the dirt in more ways than one. Butch began to work a game soon after I joined up with him which helped a bit with the funds (there wasn't any plate-passing at his revivals!) and at the same time kept up the good works. Everyone came crowding in as soon as the doors were open and packed the benches tight. It was good and warm in there. Then, when the meetings were over, we used to pile the benches out of the way and turn the hall into a doss-house without beds! It was cheaper and cleaner than most of them with, as we slung ropes from end to end of the hall at the height of a man's chest and charged a nickel

(5 c.) for the privilege of hanging over it for a night's sleep. You can still see Butch Callahan's Nickel Hang-over if you happen to be on the 'outs' in New York City. All the boys know it.

Of course, when I first went there I was amused. Then, when I had been lending a hand for a while I became interested. It didn't seem quite so funny after all, and there was work to be done, work in which, odd as it may sound, I found a measure of contentment. There wasn't anything to be made out of it and perhaps that was why. We built in a place where the boys could get a bowl of soup, or a cup of coffee and 'sinkers'. They paid when and if they could, which wasn't often.

After a while I came around to see a lot of Butch's ideas, but we just worked with different methods. He used bare knuckles, blood and hell fire, while I preferred to talk to some of them, especially the kids. I drew conclusions from my own experiences and maybe some of them listened a bit. I guess it sounds rather like the blind leading the blind but as long as I did that I managed to fight down the urge to get going again which still worries me; the longing for loose clothes once more, for the heat and the sweat and the smell of the bazaars.

I haven't got very far since I left Butch back in New York but I guess that doesn't matter a lot. The only times it worries me is when I get the wanderlust. I'm afraid it will send me 'on the run' again. I only hope I shan't grow too old this way. I'd like to die in my strength. And when I do, I daresay I shall get put alongside my old man which will give me a chance to fulfil my promise to myself and shew him that after all I went one better. Even then he may not believe me.